"This book is eloquent in its approach and elegant in its simplicity. Anyone can apply these timeless techniques to transform their relationships or any other area of life."

> –Lisa Hayes, *Author of Escape from Relationship Hell and the Host of The Relationship RX Show*

"I'm committed to families working and one thing we learn from this account of the Hawaiian Huna lineage is how to forgive family members and have life work; amazing that an ancient system would be so applicable to modern-day family life."

> –Judge Eugene M. Hyman, *recognized as an international expert in preventing juvenile, family and domestic violence*

"The power of Huna rests in the unseen, inner world. Matthew brings this world to vivid life. His deep love of his own Huna lineage allows you to touch both the deeper meaning and the practical uses of this profound Hawaiian tradition."

> –Elese Coit, *Radio host of A New Way to Handle Absolutely Everything on Contact Talk Radio*

"Dr. James has the rare ability to take you inside the secrets of Hawaiian Huna and his unique lineage. From these ancient teachings you'll learn how to ease your mind and learn to forgive, an essential element to having your brain [and life] work at its peak level."

> –Don Goewey, *stress elimination expert and best-selling author of Mystic Cool: A Proven Approach to Transcend Stress, Achieve Optimal Brain Function and Maximize Your Creative Intelligence*

"Dr. Matthew James brings the wisdom of the Huna through from 28 generations, exploring his own lineage and drawing from his experience to help others bring joy and passion to the life experience. His radiant vision is truly the link between the ancient ways of the Hawaiian elders and the seekers of our own generations."

> –Patricia Cori, *renowned author and metaphysician, is a celebrated spiritual leader, a dedicated guide to the sacred sites of the Earth, and author of the Sirian Revelations.*

THE Foundation of Huna

Ancient wisdom for modern times

MATTHEW B. JAMES, MA, PHD

www.huna.com

THE Foundation of Huna

Ancient wisdom for modern times

MATTHEW B. JAMES, MA, PHD

ADVANCED NEURO DYNAMICS, INC.
75-6099 KUAKINI HIGHWAY HI KAILUA-KONA 96740

The Foundation of Huna
Ancient Wisdom for Modern Times - 1st Edition

PUBLISHED BY Advanced Neuro Dynamics, Inc.

75-6099 Kuakini Highway
Kailua-Kona, HI 96740

ISBN: 978-0-9845107-0-2

Printed in the United States of America

NLP.com

To my Mom for introducing me to the path.

To my Dad for teaching me so much about the path.

To my Kumu Etua for taking the teachings to a deeper level.

To my wife Soomi for keeping me on track!

To my son and daughter Ethan and Skylar for showing me the future of the path.

And to all my haumana (students) who make it possible for me to teach.

Here is our beginning.

TABLE OF CONTENTS

From left to right: Etua Lopes, Uncle George Na`ope, and Matthew at the 34th Huna Workshop March 2007 in Kailua-Kona

FOREWORD

In teaching Hula dancing, I always start with the basics to bring my students to the foundation — the energy that has inspired dancers for generations. We focus on one step at a time. If you teach students one step, by the time you realize it, instead of doing five steps and sitting down, they're doing 50. Before long the students are dancing an hour and a half before they need to take a break.

It's the same in Huna, the ancient Hawaiian science of energy, consciousness and life. In Hula and Huna, a Kumu is one who teaches foundational knowledge. All foundation is consistent. A Kumu who stays connected to the foundation, stays connected to mana (energy) and can teach with authority.

In the islands today we have a young Kumu who teaches Huna from a lineage that stretches back centuries. Matthew models what he teaches with patience and perseverance, bringing students into the fullness of knowledge one step at a time.

Matthew shows how the ancient teachings of Huna empower us to discover who we are, where we come from and how to live. These teachings are written for those taking the first few steps, but they connect with traditions older than the islands and deeper than the oceans.

Because its foundations are consistent, Huna principles can benefit anyone across cultures, regardless of nationality or background. I think of the students who come from all over the world to learn Huna at our workshops in Hawai'i.

They come with their cell phones and laptops — each in his or her own little world — disconnected from the universe around them. Then after some classes and our field trips, such as the hike on the volcano, you can see them leave that box they're in as they walk into nature and embrace it. When you walk into the clouds — letting them blow into you, connecting to the trees, the wind, the quiet — you feel the connection our ancestors felt, and can tap into the source of their knowledge.

1

As they connect — with themselves, the universe, the ancient spirit — I see them change through the course of our workshops. As they let go, their true beauty shines. It's like they are breathing again.

As the Kumu Hula at Hulihe'e Palace and a student of the late Uncle George Na'ope, I have watched Matthew grow as a ho'opa'a (drummer) and chanter in Hula since 1997. I am privileged to be the godfather of Skylar, Matthew's daughter. In the 20 years I have taught in Huna workshops, I have watched as he has opened himself to become a teacher for the ancient ways.

Matthew has been entrusted with his lineage by his elders who authorized him to teach knowledge and long kept secrets. Matthew's father, Tad James, learned the wisdom from David "Papa" Bray, Jr., who had learned it from his father, David "Daddy" Bray, a Kahuna in Kailua-Kona. Papa Bray gave permission to Matthew's father to carry on the Huna lineage and teach it here in Kona. You will learn more about this lineage and how Huna has survived despite persecution; including, being at one time outlawed in Hawai'i.

Matthew began learning Huna at the age of 13 and has studied with individuals such as Uncle George. While using the most modern methods to teach Huna, Matthew has remained true to his lineage as he shares the ancient knowledge,

just as he has in the workshops we have taught together for years.

As you read these pages, you will learn that Huna is about empowering yourself, rather than fixing others. As you devote time to studying the ancient knowledge, you become like the tip of a spear, always moving forward. The deeper you go, the more you understand that you are the channel for the flow of energy. Like Hula dancers giving themselves over to the energy and rhythm, you will feel and better understand your connection to the universe.

Huna is a powerful word for me because it pertains to the whole cycle of life. The universe is our classroom. Yet in today's society, it's so hard for us to become dedicated. With everything pulling at us, it almost feels like a chore.

We must relearn how to connect with the world — with the here and now — taking the time to be in the moment, to breathe, to connect and dedicate one's self to learning. There is no dedication without sacrifice, and no sacrifice without dedication. This is the path to knowledge.

I teach my Hula students to dance with total dedication. This kind of dedication, which we call ke ike, requires you to know yourself and understand your motivations. Huna empowers you with this knowledge by both personalizing your sacredness and revealing what is obscure.

Whether you are chanting, dancing Hula, building a canoe or working as a corporate executive, Huna allows you to fully dedicate yourself. It also gives you freedom in your relationships with yourself and others, as Matthew shows, so practically, in his teachings on Ho'oponopono.

It takes a lifetime to learn. Fortunately, life is our classroom. But we each must decide, "Do I live it, or wing it?" Everything connects. Huna teaches us to see the connections, such as the connection between a sign and what we are meant to do.

Uncle George always said, "When you dance on stage, you don't dance 100 percent. You dance 200 percent. That way when you walk off the stage, you never turn around and look at the stage and say, 'I should have done that.'"

I can teach anybody Hula, but how can I make them understand what they're doing in seven or nine or 10 days? All I can do is give them a sense of direction. Through their own dedication, it's up to the students to learn what is below that.

Huna, like Hula, is about learning the traditions. You are learning sacred things, but it's more personal. What you get out of it depends on your dedication. Rather than thinking about what you are doing tomorrow, ask yourself, "What am I doing today? Am I dedicated?"

Matthew's years of study, teaching and practical application exemplify his commitment to his lineage and to sharing the deep and resilient teachings of Huna. This book is the product of his complete dedication. And it is only the beginning.

–ETUA LOPES

Etua Lopes, a student of the late Uncle George Na'ope, is the Kumu Hula at Hulihe'e Palace. Matthew has been a student of Hula with Etua since 1997.

INTRODUCTION

Matthew B. James, MA, PhD

When I was growing up, I was exposed to a wide variety of spiritual paths. I went to Catholic high school. I was baptized Presbyterian. I went to Vacation Bible School at a Protestant church for my summer fun. My mother taught transcendental meditation and my father practiced siddha yoga. My stepfather was Buddhist. My two best friends were Jewish and Muslim. I had the privilege of celebrating many of their religious holidays.

I was really confused.

To an outsider, this upbringing seemed ideal. People who felt they'd had a single philosophy crammed down their throats always told me how fortunate I was. But a wide spectrum of paths can be simply confusing for a kid.

One night, while sitting alone on my bed, I remember looking up and asking, "God, Yahweh, Jehovah, Allah, whoever is up there, just show me the path. Whichever one, and I will do it." I waited, and waited, and waited. It took a couple of decades, but I finally found the path of Huna.

I have always loved Huna, but even when you love something, there were times on the path when you question yourself and your purpose. I have been there, and I have found myself stalled in my progression down the path. And if you stall in life, the universe will figure out a way to push you down the path that is waiting for you.

Maybe that's why you picked up this book. Maybe the universe is nudging you toward the path of Huna – or maybe you're just curious. Whatever your motivation, it's fair to let you know a little about me, your tour guide on this journey.

My Story

I started exploring consciousness at a very young age, learning to meditate at age five from my mom and studying siddha yoga directly from teachers like Baba Muktananda while I was still in grade school. When I was a teenager, I got to study with human potential greats like Tony Robbins and Richard Bandler, and I became a Master Trainer in neuro linguistics in my twenties. I continued on the quest, pursuing advanced degrees in organizational development, hypnotherapy, and finally a PhD in Health Psychology.

But the thread that held it all together for me was Huna.

Uncle George Na'ope

As a young adult I studied at the feet of Uncle George Na'ope who has been named by the State of Hawai'i as a *Golden Living Treasure*. In

1963, Uncle George founded the Merrie Monarch Festival, an annual event that celebrates and perpetuates the traditional art forms and culture of Hawai'i. He explained to me that he taught the ancient teachings even when no one wanted to hear about them, even the Hawaiian people. Among other things, Uncle George has taught me concepts about Hawaiiana (the culture and mores of the islands) and spirituality. I also continue to study with one of Uncle George's well-known students Etua Lopes, who has the honor of teaching at Hulihe'e Palace on the island of Hawai'i.

David "Papa" Bray, Jr. (the son of one of the last practicing Kahuna, David "Daddy" Bray) instructed my father, Tad James, in his family's system of Huna. Papa Bray wanted to share this information with someone to preserve the lineage because he had no one in his own family who was interested in learning the material. So in the late 1980's, he gave my father and Laura Yardley permission to learn, practice and teach the Huna of the Bray family. They were charged with carrying on his lineage.

Because of my experience with mediation, or maybe because I have always felt a calling to these types of teachings, I began learning from my father the basics and advanced techniques of Huna in the early 80's while still a teenager. Some of my early lessons were at the kitchen table, and it truly became a part of my life and the way I approach everything I do.

The Bray lineage of Huna comes from Kailua-Kona. Contributing to our system of Huna are people like the late Uncle George, an expert in the chants and hula; the late John Ka'imikaua with the lineage of Moloka'i specializing in the culture, hula and spirituality; Taneo Sands Kumalae, who focuses on working with things outside you to affect change inside you; the late Morrnah Simeona, who taught my father Ho'oponopono; as well as the Bray family, the source of most of our teaching of Huna. Through the years, all of these people either taught my father or taught me. With their support and permission, I started teaching Huna in 1998. In 2005, the Bray lineage was entrusted to me. It is this lineage that I teach now at our Huna trainings.

I mention my lineage, predecessors and mentors because Uncle George taught me how important it is to respect your lineage. "When chanting, all the people in your lineage stand up behind you and chant through you," he said. "Occasionally you will feel that." And I have felt that, not only in my chanting but in my teaching. It's a deep, humbling sense that this lineage I so respect lines up behind me and my living mentors to support us as we share the ancient wisdom. I also mention my lineage because unlike some of the other things I teach, this is a part of my family and something I grew up with and go home to. I am committed to teaching the Huna tradition, fully and undiluted, to as many students as are called to it.

SOMETHING OLD, SOMETHING NEW

But though the Huna I teach remains true to the ancient teachings, we teach it in a thoroughly modern way. I'm pretty sure that those who came before me would have approved. Uncle George has explained numerous times at our Huna workshop that Hawaiians have always loved and employed technology. The Iolani Palace on the island of O'ahu was fully wired with electricity even before the White House!

Some of the people who have taught us studied with people who were practicing the ancient ways in remote locations. They had a direct connection to the ancient teachings that you don't find in many places across the planet.

But in ancient times if you wanted to learn how to connect with the water element, to flow the water element and to call the water element to you, you would stand on the beach at the place where the water is about knee deep. According to Uncle George, you would oli (chant) your name to the water until the water chanted your name back. This was the first part of the introduction – and it could take quite a while. When the water finally chanted back to you, you were expected to chant to the water spontaneously. You would keep at it until the water chanted its name back to you. At that point, you knew the water and you had become a master of the water element!

Uncle George said that this process took anywhere from seven years to a lifetime – if you were lucky.

Modern methods of teaching Huna allow students to connect more easily to the elements and flow the energy much more quickly. We've sped up the ancient process without compromising the ancient values and principles. We bring cutting edge psychological approaches to teaching and learning with the ancient concepts of Huna, so students are able to fully experience the process in a rapid manner. We have been teaching it this way since the late 1980's in Kailua-Kona, where our lineage is based.

HOW DOES IT RELATE TO YOU?

Huna is not just a set of esoteric principles to be practiced in remote regions of volcanic ash, dramatic waterfalls and lush tropical rain forests. I am committed to sharing the basic concepts of Huna (how to connect our three selves, to interact with the five elements and balance universal energies) because I have experienced for myself the value you receive when you apply them in your daily life, to enhance who you are and what you are doing. Huna means nothing unless it can be woven into your real-world, modern life existence. The most profound esoteric teachers I've known never told us to abandon what we have, what we do, or who we are. Instead, they encourage us to embrace the precious nuggets of the ancient wisdom and incorporate these nuggets, fully integrate them, into our current realities.

The majority of ancient Hawaiians fully integrated concepts such as aloha, personal responsibility, and cause and effect into their lives (principles that also form the basis of Huna). They created a society that, prior to the arrival of the missionaries, was virtually free of physical and psychological disease. The name Hawai'i itself expresses how fully enmeshed spiritual life has been to this culture. As taught by Uncle George, we can see the deeper meaning of the word Hawai'i when we break down its syllables: According to Uncle George, Ha means "breath;" wai can be translated as "water" or mana which is "life force" or "energy;" i means "Supreme". Combined, Hawai'i means "the Supreme life force that rides on the breath."

Hawai'i, a powerful, spiritual name for a powerful, spiritual culture.

Chapter One: Huna Overview

Huna is not a religion, but an integrated system of energy work, psychology, and spirituality. It is not meant to replace your own religion or beliefs but to enhance them. Huna is one of the original sciences of healing, enlightenment and personal empowerment. It taught people how to get in touch with their mana (life-force energy), how to move this energy, and how to understand their individual connection with the environment and with others. It instructed them on how energy moved back and forth between them and everything else around them.

All ancient Hawaiians knew and lived by the basic concepts of Huna: cause and effect, perception is projection, and responsibility for change. They didn't see these concepts as complex theories that should be studied. Rather they saw Huna fundamentals just as the reality of how things work, simply the way that nature and consciousness operate. It's similar to the way you and I think about gravity or the way the sun moves across the sky. Most of us don't understand in depth how gravity works or the rotation of the earth, but we understand just enough to be pretty clear about what will happen if we step out of a fifteenth floor window! And we know that it would be silly to be shocked, surprised, or upset when the sun turns in for the night. It's just the way things work. And so it was with ancient Hawaiians and Huna fundamentals.

What's in a Name?

Huna (as a name for the concepts I teach) is a modern or Western label given to this ancient system, but according to Papa Bray, the system was originally called Ho'omana. Ho'o means "to make" and mana means "life force," equivalent to ki (as in Aikido), chi (as in Tai Chi) or shakti in the Sanskrit language. Taken together the word Ho'omana means empowerment or to empower.

Simply translated, the word huna means secret. The story goes that Max Freedom Long, one of the first Westerners to investigate Huna and write about it in the early 20th century, asked the Hawaiians, "This system of esoteric studies that you have over here, what is it?" They replied, "That is huna, shhhhh," which Long assumed to be the system's title.

But the Hawaiians were trying to tell him that the ancient system and its fundamentals were "secret." Not secret in the sense that no one knew about them, because Huna basics were well known. They meant secret in the sense of knowledge which is concealed from the casual observer, wisdom which is protected like a treasure or a science that is esoteric and difficult to really understand at depth.

Auntie Bernie Konanui

Auntie Bernie Konanui (Uncle George Na'ope's sister) explained to me that while some people believe the current use of the label Huna is inaccurate, in ancient times the word described a state of being or a state of consciousness. She agrees with others, as do I, that what I teach today was not called Huna in ancient Hawai'i. In fact, to teach it means that it is no longer secret, no longer huna.

However, she said that when a person was able to block out the surface level clutter and noise of daily existence and delve into the deeper secret of an issue or problem to solve it, they would be described as having the huna, the ability to find the concealed wisdom. Auntie Bernie explained that most people are unable to find this deeper meaning or hidden wisdom. But those who do find it are empowered and able to find success and happiness in life. This is a fundamental concept of the Huna teachings.

Personally, I believe we spend too much time debating labels. While I could argue both sides of whether we should call it Huna or not, the more important consideration is what I teach rather than the name I use. Called Ho'omana, Huna, or any other label used in ancient times, it would still be the same teachings. I focus more on those teachings themselves.

THE BIG KAHUNA

Just as there are some folks today who understand the intricacies of gravity and underlying logic of the movement of the solar system, ancient Hawai'i had experts who deeply understood and worked with the underlying science of Huna. They were known as the Kahuna.

Do you remember the Big Kahuna in the Frankie Avalon, Annette Funicello movies in the late 60's? The Big Kahuna was the guy who was terrific at surfing. He knew secrets about surfing that other surfers didn't know and could do amazing things on a surfboard other surfers couldn't seem to do. He was absolutely the best! Though Big Kahuna was a tongue-in-cheek title in those movies, it pretty closely reflects what the word means.

Ka means "the," or "light," and we know that Huna means "secret" or esoteric. If we divide the word differently (which is a really common practice in discovering the deeper meanings of Hawaiian words), Kahu means "keeper", "honored servant" or "high servant who takes charge of persons, property, or knowledge." Na means "to care for," "to settle difficulties, in a legal sense;" "quiet, pacified, as an aggrieved child;" "calmed, quieted, as one's passions, calm and centered."

You can think of a Kahuna as being roughly equivalent to PhD., a learned specialist in a particular field. When I asked Uncle George if the PhD comparison was correct, he said "Yeah. But it wouldn't be just any PhD. It would be the one who was considered the best doctor in that area, like the best oncologist in northern California." In ancient times, there were Kahuna of fishing, farming, and planting, and Kahuna of philosophy, negotiation, and government. There were Kahuna of canoe building and navigation, and Kahuna of child birthing and rearing. If you wanted to learn to carve statues, you could go to a Kahuna of tiki (statues). If you wanted to learn hula you would go to a Kahuna of the hula.

There were also Kahuna who studied the fundamentals of Ho'omana then specialized in its different aspects: Kahuna called La'au Lapa'au specialized in physical healing; predictors or those who did divination were called Kilokilo; La'au Kahea were experts at psychological healing and had the ability to call the mana or energy; and mystical initiators were called Na'auao. These are the four main aspects that Papa Bray shared with my father as an explanation of the Bray family Huna. There were many powerful teachings in the family, but my main focus is on teaching Ho'omana or empowerment.

THE BRIEF STORY OF A LONG HISTORY

We believe that the origins of the ancient sciences and arts now called Huna may be as old as 35,000 years. According to traditional teachings, Huna originated from the original teachings of the peoples of the earth who were centered in Hawai'i on a continent which no longer exists. All that remains physically of that land are the mountain peaks of the island chain called Hawai'i.

From their very beginning until approximately 750 A.D., these original teachings flourished as a system of personal development, healing, and spiritual discipline that was known by all people. It was a balanced system, one that honored men and women equally. The knowledge and wisdom that comprised the original teachings weren't organized or formally taught. They were passed on verbally and formed the basic foundation for understanding the workings of nature and consciousness.

There are only remnants of this original system around the earth. Starting in 325 A.D. (it may have started as early as several thousand years B.C., but the effects were definitely under way by 325 A.D.), an attempt to destroy the feminine/masculine balanced systems of the original teachings of the peoples of the earth engulfed the planet. Before 750 A.D., Uncle George explained that the balanced order existing in Hawai'i was a system called The Order of Kane. Other balanced systems flourished all over the world. In India, the system was Tantra and Native American Indian cultures, the Maori of New Zealand, and Aboriginal peoples of Australia all lived within such balanced systems. The system in Western Europe which worshipped both a God and a Goddess was called Wicca.

But a wave swept over the planet to wipe these balanced systems out. The Spanish Inquisition (which followed a papal inquisition in other parts of Europe) conducted by a Catholic tribunal reduced the population of Spain by more than 50% in 200 years, killing hundreds of thousands of people and nearly extinguishing Wicca. In India, the new system of Vedanta attempted to replace Tantra. Although Tantra fared better than Wicca, both systems were subjected to relentless persecution. The situation was the same all over the world, and each of the peoples bearing the original teachings were (and still are) subjected to the intentional eradication of their culture and teachings.

This wave hit Hawai'i sometime between 750 and 1250 A.D. According to Uncle Geroge, at that time the warrior Pa'ao arrived in Hawai'i from Tahiti and found a very peace-loving people living in a paradise. Several years later, Pa'ao returned with a number of warriors and priests and overturned the original system in Hawai'i. When Pa'ao arrived, he installed the system or Order of Ku, a system that was very male-dominated, and the original teaching was changed. The old order was overturned.

The Huna that we teach predates the teaching of Pa'ao. So it is very ancient, from before 750 A.D. But because Huna was an oral tradition, there are conflicting chants about how long ago this occurred and the specifics of the story. Fortunately, when the original teachings in Hawai'i were overturned, they went underground. The teachings were hidden within the chants of the Ancient Ones and the Hulahula (hula dances). Though the newer arrivals adopted Hawaiian chants and Hulahula, followers of Ku remained ignorant of the original mysteries hidden within.

The teachings were buried in the chants to a deeper second level when missionaries arrived from Boston in 1820. King Kamehameha II and Queen Ka'ahumanu, his stepmother, had already abolished the old system or kapu (taboo) system of religious laws in 1819 by disbanding priestly orders and destroying all of their temples and sacred images. So the missionaries' arrival was very timely. They brought with them their Christian God and mores, and sought to ban the old "superstitious ways." In 1820, the first of several laws designed to eradicate the ancient teachings were passed:

"Section 1034: Sorcery – Penalty, Any person who shall attempt the cure of another by the practice of sorcery, witchcraft, ananna (sic), hoopiopio, hoounauna, or hoomanamana, or other superstitious or deceitful methods, shall, upon conviction thereof, be fined in a sum not less than one hundred dollars or be imprisoned not to exceed six months at hard labor.' There is also another section of the law which classes the kahuna with bunco men and defines him as one posing as a kahuna, taking money under pretense of having magical power, or admitting he is a kahuna. For this the fine goes up to a thousand dollars and a year in prison." [1]

---

1 James, T. (1997). The Lost Secrets of Ancient Hawaiian Huna. Honolulu, HI: Advanced Neuro Dynamics.

Thus Hawaiians were prevented from practicing their original teachings until the federal government of the United States passed the Native American Religious Freedoms Act in 1979. As late as 1953, a Kahuna, Daddy Bray, was arrested for chanting a chant in the Hawaiian language at Hulihe'e Palace in downtown Kailua-Kona – a chant quite similar to a chant we now teach at our Huna seminars in Hawai'i. Some believe that the final law in Hawai'i against the practice of the ancient ways was repealed in 1989.

Shamanism is broadly defined as disciplines that connect the spiritual world with the physical.

So there's been a huge time gap between the period when Huna was practiced openly and the revival of this knowledge. The key people involved in keeping the arts, sciences and wisdom of Huna alive besides the Bray family lineage are people like Uncle George Na'ope, John Ka'imikaua, Max Freedom Long, Serge King (who carries a Huna lineage of Kauai) and countless other Hawaiians who preserve the teachings and the concepts. I offer a heartfelt thank you to all of them.

HUNA AND SHAMANISM

Shamanism is broadly defined as disciplines that connect the spiritual world with the physical. The similarities between Huna and other shamanistic paths indicate that the origins of Huna are the same as Wicca, alchemy, or Hermetics in western Europe, Native American traditions, Aboriginal teachings in Australia, the Maori teachings in New Zealand, and the original teaching of Tantra in India.

For example, Hermetics, alchemy, and Native American traditions all acknowledge the Holy Guardian Spirit which corresponds to Huna's higher self. Hermetics, alchemy and the Tantra of India are all based on five elements as is Huna. Native American, Maori, and Aboriginal traditions embrace Dream Time which is comparable to the Moemoea (dream time or rare dream) in Hawai'i. Huna shares a tradition of using herbs for healing with Native Americans and Chinese, and energy healing practice with Reiki practitioners and healers in the Philippines. Kahuna use clouds, numbers and the stars to make predictions in ways similar to traditions in astrology, the Kabalah, and numerology. Chanting is commonly used by Native Americans, the Maori, in Tantra and in Huna.

Of course, there would be similarities between Huna and the other shamanistic disciplines if they all sprang from the same origin. But while most, if not all, of the components of the other major esoteric disciplines have been written and published, more than 80% of what is really Huna has not yet been published.

There were two major bodies of teachings that Papa Bray taught my father. One was the ho'omana which is taught to the public. The other, which is practitioner work or an integrated life path, has not yet been taught to the public. While the foundation for the deeper teachings has been created with some of the long term haumana (students) of our Huna workshop, the teaching has not yet begun.

THE BASIS OF THE SCIENCE OF HUNA

We will delve into the various aspects of the art and science of Huna throughout this book. But the following chant represents the overall underlying intention of Huna:

E iho ana o luna

E pi'i ana o lalo

E hui ana na moku

E ku ana ka paia

"Bring down that which is above by means of the light. To ascend take from darkness into light that which is below by means of the light.

This will transform the spiritual energy as it flows from the source and integrates all the islands (inside you), giving peace.

This will affect you profoundly, and change your life bringing illumination, and you will feel the delightful supreme fire."

–Kapihe (Kahuna, 1850, Kona, HI) [2]

This chant echoes teachings in other esoteric traditions:

"That which is above is like that which is below, and that which is below is like that which is above."

–Hermes Trismegistus from the *Law of Correspondence in the Emerald Tablet*, circa 1500 AD [3]

"And 144 (thousand) light warriors with their shields balanced, respecting all paths as leading to one shall come to the planet in her time of need and teach the teachers."

–Hopi Legend [4]

SUMMARY:

1. Huna is not a religion but an ancient system that explains the nature of reality and consciousness.

2. Huna shares its origins and many of its tenets with teachings of other ancient cultures and peoples.

3. Huna is both an esoteric system and a practical approach to daily life.

———————

2, 3, 4 James, T. (1997). *The Lost Secrets of Ancient Hawaiian Huna. Honolulu, HI: Advanced Neuro Dynamics.*

Chapter Two: Aloha

Even if you've never visited the islands, you're probably familiar with the word aloha. Most people think of it as a greeting, but the word only became a greeting around the time the American missionaries arrived. Today, aloha kakahiaka can be translated as "good morning;" aloha awakea means "good afternoon" and aloha ahiahi means "good evening." There's another level of meaning in this greeting according to Uncle George: alo means "goes with you" and ha is "breath" and breath is life. So when a person says aloha to you, they are saying "my breath goes with you." As essential as the breath is, this explains why aloha has so many meanings. Aloha shares its root with the Maori greeting aroha and would be similar to the deeper meaning of other common salutations such as namasté, shalom, adieu, and salaam.

Aloha also means "from the heart." It means love, compassion, affection, peace and mercy.

In local slang, or the combination of English and Hawaiian locally, you could say "I aloha you" to mean "I love you" or mea aloha to mean "loved one" or "beloved." Aloha ke akua is "love of God" and aloha makua is to be loving and considerate of elders. Almost every kumu (teacher) I've had says that you have to come from a place of aloha when you do anything, but especially when you share knowledge. They say you must teach from the heart, and you have to accept and malama (cherish) everyone around you. Daddy Bray said that Huna responds to your aloha. He said that Huna or life energy flows best when your focus and intention comes from the heart.

Native Hawaiians know that there is even more to aloha when you look below surface definitions. Papa Bray taught my father the secret meaning of aloha that healers and Kahuna in ancient times knew. This secret meaning of aloha was the basis for how they behaved. This deeper meaning is found within each letter and it represents a state of mind, an agreed-upon set of values and a way of being in the world. This level of aloha includes many of the basic principles of Huna, so I begin with aloha as an introduction to and overview of the concepts I'll share in more depth throughout this book.

> Almost every kumu (teacher) I've had says that you have to come from a place of aloha when you do anything, but especially when you share knowledge.

A = AO AND ALA

1. AO or Light: Huna says that all of our behavior should move us toward the light. We should maintain watchful alertness so our actions lead others and ourselves in the direction of the light (enlightenment) with watchful alertness. The question we must always ask is, "Does my behavior lead me toward earth-ing my energy or toward enlightenment?"

Ao is the light. In life there is the dark and the light. David "Daddy" Bray had a different approach to Huna than many other practitioners. He recognized the dichotomies (or opposites), and did not shy away from them. He did not deny there were bad things in life. He just said that you have a choice. When his son Papa Bray

explained this to my father, he said that we all have a choice, no exceptions. Most of us know that we have choice, though at times we'd prefer not to admit it. But it's clear that some people in a bad economy still find a way to tap into their own resources and thrive. Others in the same situation blame their personal circumstance or the economy and struggle to survive. The difference is that individuals who thrive realize at some level that they have choice in how they experience the world, including choice regarding issues like prosperity. Ao says that you need to choose and work with the light to progress down a spiritual path.

2. ALA or To look: Ho'o ao means "to look for right time and right place." To pay attention to what's happening around you and to look outside yourself. Doing so leads to behavior that is circumscribed and appropriate for all occasions. Someone who does not ho'o ao may speak inappropriately, act silly or simply talk when they should be listening. People interested in themselves only like to overwhelm us. People who are interested in what is around them will listen to us. Huna asks us to look around, take everything in, and pay attention! If you do, you will know whether the timing is right to say what you have to say out loud or not.

L = LOKAHI

Oneness: Oneness among us and with all things. All is one. And because all is one, Huna says that we must always seek to be pono with ourselves, one another, and our world. Pono means to be "right," but not in the sense of right versus wrong. Pono is the sense of being aligned, in perfect order, clear. Pono is a deep sense of well-being. Because I am you and you are me, when I harm you, I am harming myself. When I reject you, I reject myself. Anything less than 100% support of one another sabotages both of us. Because we are not perfect, becoming pono with ourselves, each other and our world is a constant, active process.

Lokahi means oneness as well as working with unity. It's a word that's being used a lot in Hawai'i right now when referring to groups coming together. But in Huna, one of lokahi's most important aspects is unity within yourself.

Lokahi is acceptance of self on all levels: conscious, unconscious, and higher self. It emphasizes the importance unifying all of our selves within our lives, respecting our physical bodies, listening to our intuition, allowing guidance from a higher self. The best decisions are made using conscious thought, unconscious alignment and higher self energy. To lokahi is to use all three, rather than just one.

O = 'OIA'I'O

Truth or to tell the truth: 'Oia'i'o means to be genuine or authentic, truthful. Most of us are too polite or too frightened to tell each other the truth. We may not be intentionally or blatantly dishonest, yet we hold back a part of ourselves or withhold our true thoughts. We pretend to be okay when we aren't. We feign agreement to avoid potential unpleasantness. Huna says that these actions prevent us from fully participating in the process of constructing our universe. Without authenticity, we can't have oneness. We are prevented from being truly pono with ourselves or anyone else.

So 'oia'i'o is more than just a great Scrabble word. (Forward and backward: Bonus points!) It's a concept that I have really taken to heart and it has served me well. In Western society, it's so easy to tell white lies. (By the way, no matter what color you make it, a lie is still a lie!) I believe in being kind, loving and caring to everyone. But I made the decision as I began to teach Huna that I would be truthful and honest. If someone asks me a direct question, I give a direct answer. Sometimes a person will ask a question, and I have to tell them the truth: that I would prefer not to answer that question!

It's a simple, though not always easy, rule to follow. Just be truthful. If I don't know the answer to a question, I say that I don't know. 'Oia'i'o isn't just about being truthful with others but also with yourself. Practicing 'oia'i'o brought up my fears about relationship because this truthfulness catapulted my relationships to a completely new level.

This is the level where my wife and I play in our aloha. This is how we live. For example, years ago I led a practitioner training in Toronto and someone asked me a health question. My response simply flowed and I felt good as I got off stage. I asked my wife, Soomi, what she thought about the session. She said "Yes, it was really good information. May I give you some feedback?" She went on to explain that though the information was there, it felt like a contradiction because I was not applying it to myself. I was 65 pounds heavier than I am today. She said, "I married you, and I love you for who you are. But you've gotten up on stage and explained that people can't teach others how to quit smoking if they haven't done it themselves." Her level of caring and truthfulness sparked in me the motivation to get back in shape and personify physically what I was teaching about health.

Some people hear that story and think what she said was unkind and unnecessary. For me, I wouldn't want her to be any other way. It is simply a deeper level of honesty. When we have this level of honesty with another person, it deepens our relationship immeasurably. When we have this level of honesty with ourselves, it brings us closer to Keawe, Source.

H = HA'A HA'A

Humility or to be humble: Ha'a ha'a is a very important concept in Huna and on any path to expanding awareness. Ego is a big trap along the road of spiritual evolution. The minute you think you know something for certain, you're ruined in spiritual matters. The ego also prevents you from telling the truth. When you play the game of power, you lose your connection to others and your openness to deeper wisdom and learning. The game of showing off to "prove" yourself to others will never be truly satisfying.

One of my favorite sayings is "You never know who you're talking to." The person listening to you may know more about a topic than you do but will listen to you to see what you really know. The more I've learned, the more I realize how much I don't know and how much there is to learn. Being ha'a ha'a is offering respect to everyone and respecting where they came from in their model of the world.

If a person asks me what I do for a living and we talk at depth, I'll eventually explain about Huna because I want to be truthful. However, I don't start off by saying that I lead Huna trainings, that I can flow energy, and that I've got several degrees in various disciplines. That's not being ha'a ha'a. To be ha'a ha'a, I give the easiest, simplest explanation that is truthful. "I work with individuals on improving what they do. I work with individuals on their communication skills. I teach people to empower themselves."

But to be humble does not mean to hide your light or pretend to be less than you are. That is a false humility that serves no one. Ha'a ha'a says, "I know I have gifts, as do others. I have things to teach, and much to learn. My talents are to be shared, not applauded."

The more you offer and share with others, the more comes back to you. The more you appreciate rather than seeking to be appreciated, the more and more energy returns to you. Huna asks us to remember to remain humble. If you think you know more than others, then you'll have to prove it. And the minute you have to prove it, it becomes power and the minute it's power, then it's not the last "A" which is:

A = ALOHA AND AHONUI

Aloha: absolute, true love. Aloha includes compassion, mercy and kindness. Aloha does not make comparisons or judgments nor does it grade others. It does not discriminate or judge people spiritually. When we judge, compare or discriminate, we separate ourselves from true love. In that moment, we give up the spark of divine essence that comes from pure spirit, the love that we are, all of us. The minute we make comparisons, we're not ha'a ha'a. Elizabeth Kubler Ross, the psychiatrist famous for her teachings about death and dying, wrote: "Before you go you're going to be asked: Did you love enough? Did you learn enough?"

Ahonui: patient perseverance. Besides aloha, the final A also represents ahonui. Ahonui is patient perseverance. Back in the 1960's, Daddy Bray said that we live in a world that moves so fast that we expect things to come to us instantaneously. I think that is even more accurate today in our drive-through/google-based/ Twitter-happy/microwave culture. I do believe that you can create instantaneously, especially things like shifting your state and changing your feelings. But I believe that a body of work or knowledge like Huna requires a lifetime—and patient perseverance.

LET'S BEGIN

Every journey, whether for a lifetime or a few hours, begins with one step and continues step by step. Over the next pages, I will take you on a step-by-step journey through the basics of Huna. And, as we progress, keep in mind the teachings of aloha because, as Auntie Bernie once told me, what you put into Huna is what you get back. Huna is a powerful set of tools that needs to be guided by aloha and your heart.

SUMMARY:

Fundamentals of Huna include:

Light: We can choose to move toward the light.

Awareness: Paying attention to all that is around us.

Oneness: All is one.

Truth: To be authentic with ourselves and others.

Humility: To be open and teachable.

Love: Unconditional love for self and others.

Persistence: To have patient perseverance.

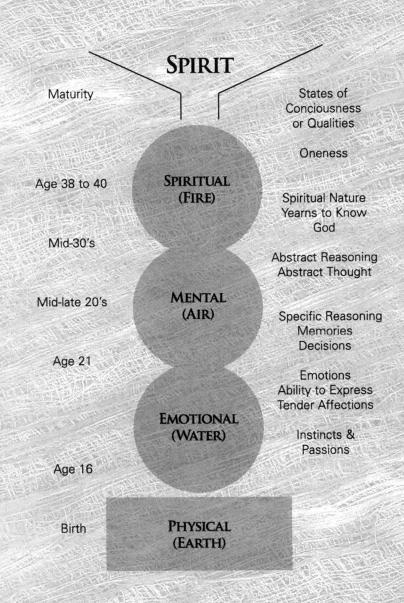

SPIRIT

Maturity

States of
Conciousness
or Qualities

Oneness

Age 38 to 40

SPIRITUAL
(FIRE)

Spiritual Nature
Yearns to Know
God

Mid-30's

Abstract Reasoning
Abstract Thought

Mid-late 20's

MENTAL
(AIR)

Specific Reasoning
Memories
Decisions

Age 21

Emotions
Ability to Express
Tender Affections

EMOTIONAL
(WATER)

Instincts &
Passions

Age 16

Birth

PHYSICAL
(EARTH)

CHAPTER THREE: OUR FOUR BODIES

According to what Papa Bray taught my father, in the ancient Hawaiian system there was a physical body, emotional body, mental body and a spiritual body. Papa said that each body is progressively larger than the last. Each body layers on top of the other, thereby expanding the overall body. Your spiritual body is the final, outer-most layer. In other systems, this spiritual body might be labeled as an aura or your energy field. But if everything is within one energy field as quantum physics has discovered, then these four bodies are merely four different aspects, components or vibrational levels of one energy.

INFINITE TO FINITE

Imagine yourself as an infinite being of light with infinite wisdom, floating in the cosmos. Suddenly, your cosmic cell phone rings. You check caller ID and see that it's the Creator on the line. (So you figure you'd better answer it before it goes into voicemail!) Before even saying "Whass'up?" She tells you, "You're going to earth."

According to the book The Lost Secrets of Ancient Hawaiian Huna Vol 2 by my father Tad James and Uncle George Na'ope, the Hawaiians have a specific chant that describes the experience of the light/spirit returning to the earth: No luna e ka hale kai. The chant says that as the light comes streaming across the po (deep nothingness), it looks like a seedling of light. The end of the chant says: I laila ho i ("seedlings of light come back to me"). As an infinite being of light, you go streaming across po headed toward earth. When you come into physical manifestation, it's as though you are being squeezed through a tube of toothpaste. Then suddenly, wham! You've got a physical body.[1]

---

1 As an aside, Uncle explained that there are multiple translations for chants, largely based on the context. For the hula you would have one translation about the actual story of No Luna, but a spiritual context might have a very different meaning. Neither was right or wrong he said, but a part of the culture.

You also have an emotional body, mental body and spiritual body. Papa explained that you have all four bodies at birth. You are an infinite being of light that has been funneled into human existence. In Huna, our individual spiritual growth requires us to develop and fully integrate functioning of each of the bodies, as each body develops and matures. Since each body matures at a different age, all are not available for development at the same time. But as a person matures, each body becomes available to be developed and integrated.

THE STAGES

Generally speaking, the four bodies of most human beings go through maturation in a certain sequence at certain ages. However, there are always exceptions, and maturation is an individual process. For instance, though pre-adolescence is considered the prime time for maturation of the physical body, a very young child could also be particularly spiritual. So the chart on opposite page only indicates averages.

DEFINING MATURATION

What does maturation of these bodies mean? It's easiest to understand looking at the physical body. From a physical perspective, most of us come into maturity around the age of sixteen. We have gone through puberty and our physical body stops growing. Most physical bodies around this age are at the peak of their vitality and coming into their physical potential and strength. As "operators" of this physical body,

by this age we have a pretty good experiential sense of how it works and how to work with it.

Though the primary maturation of the childhood period is the physical body, it doesn't mean that we didn't have emotions during that phase. Obviously young children have emotions, and the hormones directing puberty make for some pretty emotional teenage years for many of us. (My wife once asked my father, "How did you get so many gray hairs?" Without hesitating, my father pointed at me and said, "Because of him." Yep, my teenage years were challenging.)

From an emotional standpoint, an adolescent might go through turbulent times at the beginning of their emotional maturation. Most of us feel that our emotions are somewhat under control by the age of twenty-one or twenty-two. We are able to maintain greater focus at that age and have a better handle on our emotional responses. That's the signal that the emotional body has reached maturity. It doesn't mean that the emotional body hadn't been present before, nor does it mean that we won't experience any emotional upset thereafter. It's simply a point in time when a core level of maturity is achieved.

The mental body matures in our mid to late 20's. At this stage of life, we are able to think objectively, make conscious decisions based on rational data, form opinions and judgments and contemplate the abstract. This is when we tend to settle into what we are going to do with our lives from a mental perspective (e.g. career).

According to both developmental psychology and Huna, we also tend to solidify many of our opinions and beliefs around this time.

Somewhere in our mid 30's, there is an awakening of the spiritual body if there wasn't such an awakening previous to that time. There's a desire to find purpose, a yearning to "know God," or an attraction to some form of higher consciousness by whatever name you call it. Carl Jung called it the collective unconsciousness. When Jung "woke up" or reached that level of maturity in his spiritual body, he was drawn to find out about and experience the collective unconsciousness.

THE FOUR BODIES

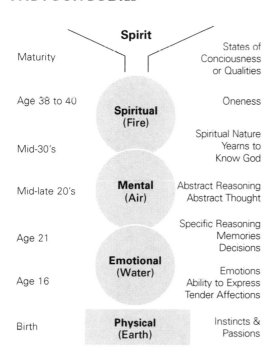

	Spirit	
Maturity		States of Conciousness or Qualities
Age 38 to 40	**Spiritual (Fire)**	Oneness
Mid-30's		Spiritual Nature Yearns to Know God
Mid-late 20's	**Mental (Air)**	Abstract Reasoning Abstract Thought
Age 21		Specific Reasoning Memories Decisions
Age 16	**Emotional (Water)**	Emotions Ability to Express Tender Affections
Birth	**Physical (Earth)**	Instincts & Passions

BODIES OUT OF BALANCE

We all know people who only experience, develop, or pay attention to the physical body. This type of person will not evolve spiritually because his focus is restricted to physical or material issues.

Other people only develop and mature in the physical and the emotional bodies. These folks will be more in touch with their emotions, yet not very intellectually developed nor spiritually aware. Some people experience just the physical and mental bodies, ignoring the emotional. These people will likely be dissociated from their feelings.

When someone does not develop one or more of the four bodies, they are unable to perform functions relating to that undeveloped body. For example, someone who does not fully develop the emotional body may be unable to express tender affection, will be incapable of feeling these emotions personally and unable to understand them in other people.

The great thinkers and healers of our time have developed all four bodies and these bodies are fully functioning. But in the average man, the physical body and the mental body are the bodies that are emphasized in Western thinking. Therefore, these tend to be the only bodies that have fully evolved. In other people in the developed parts of the world, the emotional body has matured and the mental body has grown up to be capable of functioning subjectively. However,

27

often in this scenario, the mental body is not mature enough to engage in abstract thought. It is even rarer to find abstract thought of a truly spiritual nature. Many "ideals" that apparently qualify as such are emotional in nature, lacking the foundation of the mental body and the expansiveness of the spiritual body.

FURTHER DISTINCTION

Three of the bodies can also be divided into a lower and upper. The upper spiritual body focuses on oneness while the lower spiritual body has a desire to know God. The upper mental body involves abstract reasoning and abstract thought. The lower mental body is the location of specific reasoning, decisions, and memories. In the upper emotional body, you find the ability to express tender affection and the expression of love and happiness, while instincts and passions are at the lower emotional body. The physical body is not divided into upper and lower.

WHY IS THIS IMPORTANT?

We hear a lot of talk about balance. But I believe the way most people view balance is different than the approach Huna has to the concept. To many, balance implies an end or a sense of equality between the bodies. I once told a group that Huna teaches us to find balance with the four bodies. The next day, a student was excited to tell me that he had divided the day up into four parts. He claimed that he would forever dedicate equal and balanced time to each body.

But that kind of balance is not the goal in Huna. You are not four separate bodies. You are one person with four aspects. To create harmony and balance, Huna would ask, "Are you fulfilled and developed with each aspect? How can you begin to move towards balance?" This process toward balance is not a regimented or structured series of specific steps. It is different for each person and varies within stages. It is organic, fluid and evolves more naturally rather than being forced.

SUMMARY:

1. We are all originally beings of light.

2. As we enter the physical, we have four bodies: physical, emotional, mental and spiritual.

3. Our goal is to develop each body and allow the four to be in balance.

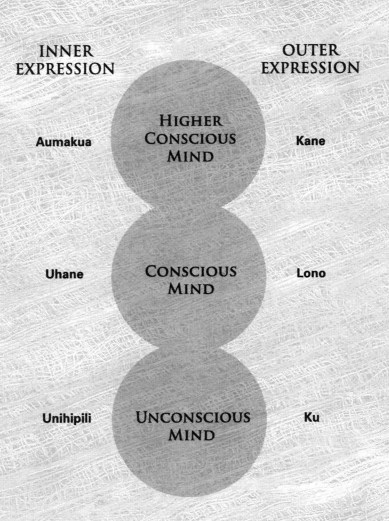

INNER
EXPRESSION

OUTER
EXPRESSION

Aumakua

HIGHER
CONSCIOUS
MIND

Kane

Uhane

CONSCIOUS
MIND

Lono

Unihipili

UNCONSCIOUS
MIND

Ku

CHAPTER FOUR: OUR THREE SELVES

Along with our four bodies, Papa Bray explained that Huna teaches that we have the three selves: conscious mind, unconscious mind and higher conscious mind. The spiritual body is related to the higher conscious mind, the mental body to the conscious mind, and the emotional body to the unconscious mind. The physical body is seen as a reflection of the other three bodies. Therefore, the physical body can be used as a gauge to measure how things are going on the other levels.

THREE, NOT TWO

When I was twelve years old, I attended my first neuro linguistic training sessions. I distinctly remember the instructor telling us, "You're a conscious mind and you're an unconscious mind and that's who you are. We're going to focus on the unconscious mind." In general, Western psychology has ignored or denied the existence of the higher consciousness or higher self, perhaps because it seems impossible to

quantify and pin down. I had already been meditating for seven years, so even at age twelve I knew intuitively that I had to be more than just my conscious and unconscious minds. I decided right then and there that I was going to figure out what the missing piece was.

Is there a higher conscious mind? Through my understanding of Huna and my studies in psychology, the easiest way to define the unconscious mind is to experience it as being anything other than the mind of which you are consciously aware (i.e. conscious mind) at any given moment. Anything that is other than your conscious and unconscious is thus considered higher consciousness.[1]

---

1 I know that many textbooks and authors refer to the unconscious mind as the sub-conscious, and I do agree that "sub-conscious" could also be the label used. But my studies and knowledge through psychology and Huna have more commonly referred to it as unconscious so I use that label here.

Besides being connected to your four bodies, all three of these minds or selves have prime directives. The three operate and communicate with the bodies and one another in particular ways. Papa Bray said that moving from unconscious mind to conscious mind to higher conscious mind is the lesson of life, and moving from higher conscious mind to conscious mind to unconscious mind is the lesson of mastery. To do this, we first need to understand our three minds or selves individually and also how they interrelate.

FIRST SELF: UHANE (CONSCIOUS MIND)

Papa Bray referred to the conscious mind as the uhane (uhane can also mean spirit). It is who you perceive yourself to be as an individual personality, how you identify yourself. Many people in modern cultures have focused solely on this aspect of self because we are so . . . well, conscious of it. It seems to be at the basis of our decisions and actions. We call on it to make judgments and solve problems. As the most tangible of our minds, the conscious mind appears to run the show.

Our conscious mind is responsible for our conscious communication and our ability to go about the day aware of our surroundings. It is the rational aspect of us, and gives us the ability to observe and experience our reality. But ancient Hawaiians knew that uhane was just one aspect of self.

SECOND SELF: UNIHIPILI (UNCONSCIOUS MIND)

The unconscious mind was called the unihipili. The literal translation of unihipili is "little creature" or "little one." If you saw something scurrying across the floor you might say, "Oh, look! An unihipili!" So the Hawaiians believed that the unconscious mind was a little self that lived inside you. Some cultures referred to the unconscious mind as the lower self. Current thinking in psychology and hypnotherapy compare characteristics of the unconscious mind with those of a 5 to 7 year-old child: simplicity, innocence, wanting to please and needing clear instruction.

Western psychology and Huna see the unconscious mind similarly in many ways. Both acknowledge that it is the unconscious that operates the body. It synchronizes breathing and heartbeat, releases hormones and regulates organ function, all with no conscious effort or attention on your part. From both a Western and Huna perspective, the unconscious also stores and organizes memories, which includes everything from remembering your own phone number to repressing memories associated with painful emotions.

But many branches of Western psychology view the unconscious as an adversary or an uncivilized child who needs taming. Western spiritual paths and philosophies often teach that we should conquer this aspect of self or purify ourselves from it in order to attain higher levels of spirituality. In contrast, ancient Hawaiians respected the wisdom of their unihipili, appreciated its contribution to their well-being, and knew it played a critical role in the connection with higher self.

UNIHIPILI AND HEALING

Within the Huna tradition, the unconscious mind is believed to have a blueprint for perfect health at the deepest level, possibly residing in the higher self. According to Uncle George, some of the first Westerners to reach Hawai'i in the 19th century found a group of people who were almost completely devoid of mental and physiological disease. Hawaiians had very little (if not zero) disease because they knew how to work with unihipili to release stress and their "stuff," the repressed emotions and memories within the unconscious mind. According to Papa Bray, the Hawaiian system of healing prior to the advent of the missionaries incorporated treatment of the entire individual, all four bodies and all three minds. It was truly a holistic or integrated approach to health and healing.

For example, the ancient Hawaiians recognized the psychological traumas associated with war, so they had specific locations where warriors would prepare for battle. When these soldiers returned from battle, they were sent to a series of healing centers. One center would heal the body, one would heal the emotions, another healed the mind, and yet another healed the spiritual body. In essence, the community de-programmed each warrior before asking him to assimilate back into his village. The Kahuna realized that asking soldiers to go home and plant crops after you'd just sent them off to kill people was a challenging transition – and not one that was likely to be successful. Instead, the system promoted full healing and total well-being.

Etua told me the story about a friend who returned from a tour of duty during the United States' first war in Iraq. "This guy came back," said Etua, "and it was as if he was still in Iraq." Many veterans have difficulty because they do not know how to work with and heal the pain stored in the unconscious after the trauma of war.

RELATING TO OUR UNIHIPILI

Your unconscious mind is like an eager child wanting to serve you and give you everything that you desire. Unihipli has only your best interests at heart and knows what it must to do to support your physical and emotional health. Yet today, many of us treat our unconscious mind abusively. We ask it for more physical energy because we want to work twelve, even fifteen hours a day. We ignore our unihipili's attempts to surface repressed pain for healing because we don't want to deal with the discomfort. We thwart the survival instincts of our unconscious by placing ourselves in dangerous or unhealthy environments. And when the unconscious mind attempts to do its job by forcing us to sleep to repair the body, presenting painful issues for resolution, or activating our fear response to keep us from risky actions, we get angry with it. We browbeat it into submission or berate ourselves for our "lack of control."

But the ancient Hawaiians were much more respectful. They understood the wisdom and responsibility of their unihipili. They also knew that their connection to their higher conscious mind, their higher self, was through the unconscious, not in spite of it.

Third Self: Aumakua (Higher Consciousness)

The higher conscious mind was called aumakua which, according to David "Papa" Bray, Jr. means "totally trustworthy parental spirit." Though higher consciousness or higher self doesn't appear in many Western psychologies, the concept of a Guardian Spirit is very common in other traditions. Ancient artists often used halos or circles of light to represent higher consciousness. A person with that halo was thought to have achieved a level where his or her higher conscious mind was always present.

Some traditions, such as that of the Native Americans, believed that you could only connect with your higher consciousness through ceremony or initiation. You had to first call to the Guardian Spirit then connect with it in specific, prescribed ways. Only then could you become one with your higher conscious mind. But Huna says you are already and always connected. However, you must work with your higher conscious mind or it will wander off and do whatever it does, waiting for you to wake up!

Higher conscious minds of people who are not awake to their spirituality need something to do. So it's as if these ignored higher conscious minds are off playing a game, maybe something like Texas Hold 'em. When one higher conscious mind says to another, "Hey, are you in for another hand?" that one looks to see what is happening with you. "Mmm, Matt's not awake yet. Yeah, deal me in." But as soon as you wake up spiritually, your higher conscious mind is fully present. You're always connected with it. It may not be easy to sense. But when you engage with it, work with it, it's always readily available.

What does "working" with aumakua mean? It means learning how to experience the connection with your inner voice. In one of his many presentations at our Huna workshop, John Ka'imikaua explained that intelligence was viewed very differently in ancient times. In modern times, we consider a person who is educated and able to think analytically as the most intelligent. But the ancient Hawaiians thought that the person who could clearly hear the inner voice or listen to the gut was more intelligent. John explained that to hear the na'au (gut) was a gift, and that this intuitive ability provides more intelligence than the mind. Since the aumakua is connected to the unconscious mind, we only hear our inner voice and guidance from aumakua through our na'au.

Of the thousands of people I have taught, we all seem to have had an experience where the gut was instructing us to proceed in a certain direction, but the head overruled that instruction and caused us to go a different direction. Invariably, we later realize that we should have listened to the gut! That was the na'au, and the aumakua giving guidance. But Western thinking tends to put more stock in the conscious, analytical, logical mind.

The goal in Huna is not to throw out our analytical cognitive ability. The goal is to learn about all three minds, and to make sure you are aligned with the conscious mind, the unconscious mind, and the higher self when doing or deciding anything. The idea is to listen respectfully to all messages that come in from any of the three minds.

When you experience higher conscious connection, perhaps receiving information, insight or a blessing, in addition to experiencing it from the na'au, you may also feel what is called ka'auhelemoa or "the rain of blessing." It feels like a fine mist which positions itself right over your head. Many students say that they experience that tingling feeling when their aumakua is present. Personally, whenever I feel that sensation, I have learned to pay particular attention to that moment.

VIEW FROM AUMAKUA

The higher self looks at you and sees you as a perfect being of light. Its prime directive is to assist you in achieving whatever it is that you want to achieve, to give you guidance, to give you mana. It would never tell you what to do. It is non-judgmental and non-demanding. It will never force you but will assist you only with guidance. It wants you to have happiness, success, love, joy, all those things that you want.

Science has now proven that aumakua's view of us is correct; we're all beings of light. According to quantum physics, at one of the deepest levels of who and what we are, we are made up of condensed light. Also, we are carbon-based life forms and carbon comes from a star (at least according to my astronomy teacher in college!). A long time ago, a star ran through the entire periodical chart, got all the way up to carbon, and then went supernova and blew carbon out. It was collected by the earth's atmosphere and became the basic building molecules of who and what we are. Trace our roots back to the stars and you find light.

HOW THE SELVES INTERRELATE

It is important to understand the way in which the three selves or minds are connected. The conscious mind is connected to the unconscious mind. The unconscious mind is connected to the higher conscious mind. This is a fundamental concept that appears in every system that I've studied around the planet. In Huna, the connection between the three selves is called an aka ("etheric substance that is a conduit for energy") connection. Through the aka connection, mana passes. So the exchange that takes place between the three selves is an energetic exchange.

Papa Bray talked about one of the lessons of life: that the conscious mind grows up to become a higher conscious mind. He said that so many people feel a yearning for spiritual teachings because the conscious mind naturally wants to become higher consciousness, to evolve to that level.

However, the conscious mind is not directly connected to the higher conscious mind. Who does the conscious mind have to work with? The unconscious mind. Therefore, one of the main lessons in life for each of us as a conscious mind is to learn to become a totally trustworthy parental spirit to our unconscious mind. Doing so opens up the channel for the energy to come in from higher consciousness.

To become that totally trustworthy parent to the unconscious, Huna says that we have to first consciously learn what the higher conscious mind does and how it relates to the unconscious. Then we must consciously model ourselves after our higher conscious mind and treat our unconscious as the higher conscious mind treats it. This opens up the energy flow from higher self to unconscious to conscious. Does that sound convoluted? Let's try an analogy.

Have you ever heard of dog whisperers? These are people who can work almost magically with dogs because they have learned canine language. They seem to have a sixth sense, a rapport that regular trainers simply don't have. What if you wanted to become a dog whisperer? You'd have to give up your normal way of relating to your dog. Initially, you would have to mimic and model the behavior of real dog whisperers to begin to communicate with your pet and to start understanding its perspective. Once you treat your pet as a dog whisperer does, your dog is able to open up and show you its language. And once you have learned its language, you really are a dog whisperer!

So it's a cyclical process. You begin by modeling the way your higher conscious mind relates to you as an individual being. When you do so, you build rapport and understanding with your unconscious mind. Then your unconscious mind relates directly with your higher self and flows its energy to your conscious self. Connecting with the higher conscious mind gets you in touch with the mana or the energy that affects your projections which creates the universe around you (we'll discuss the concept of projections in the next chapter), and being able to tap aumakua energy has the potential of making everything better.

HOW HIGHER SELF RELATES

So if we are to model how the higher conscious mind relates to the unconscious mind, what would that look like? First of all, aumakua exists in a continual state of pono, a sense of total well-being. Pono means that you are right with who you are, authentic and clear, from the outer layer of your skin all the way into the deepest part of your bone. Auntie Bernie explained that when one is pono, it is as if they have an unwavering congruency about themselves, another person, or possibly a situation. That state of pono makes everything seem right in the world. I believe that each of us has had moments when we felt this, and most of us desire to move back to that state.

The higher self also sees you and all beings as beings of pure light, including all of your bodies and all of your selves. So your higher self relates to your unconscious with perfect love, non-judgment, total appreciation.

OUTER EXPRESSION

The Hawaiians believed "as above, so below," which meant that you, as an individual, have an inner expression (above) and an outer expression (below). According to Papa Bray, the outer expressions were depicted as three gods: Ku, Lono and Kane.

Papa Bray related the unconscious mind to Ku, the impulse-driven god, and he related the conscious mind to Lono, who represented awareness, consciousness, and clarity. While these are important relationships, the most important concept for Huna is that of the higher self and the relationship to Kane.

THE THREE SELVES
PLUS MANA EQUALS FOUR (HA)

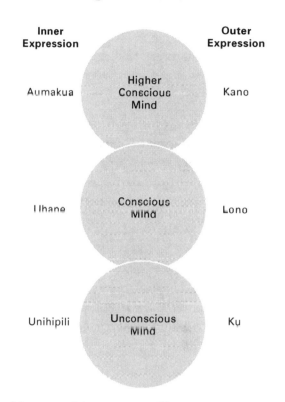

Inner Expression — Outer Expression

Aumakua — Higher Conscious Mind — Kano

I Ihane — Conscious Mind — Lono

Unihipili — Unconscious Mind — Ku

HIGHER MIND AND KANE

Your outer expression of the higher conscious mind is Kane, the Creator of the Universe. This makes sense because the inner expression, aumakua, of higher conscious mind is the creator of your personal universe. The concept of the internal and the external being reflections of one another is important. In Western thinking, we disconnect ourselves from the world around us. We believe we are separate from that which we observe, and this has led to how we treat the planet and each other. John Ka'imikaua continuously emphasized that harmony was a focus in ancient Hawai'i and the balance between akua (god, higher self, or creator), the individual and the aina (land, environment and others outside of us) was always considered before taking action.

The higher self (as below) is associated with Kane (as above) to reinforce that we each carry an aspect of the universal concept of Source or Creator. Thus we each have a level of control over our own creation of experience.

While Kane is the masculine form, in the Hawaiian system and also in the internal expression of our higher self, aumakua, there is a perfect balance of male/female energy. Though Kane is called the Creator, the creation story, Kumulipo, reveals the importance of the feminine, Na Wahine.

According to Kumulipo (the Hawaiian story of creation), Kane was in the darkness, the nothingness called the po. Kane was as if dead in the kingdom of po until receiving the kisses of Na Wahine, the feminine aspect. In the ancient teachings of Huna, the women in the Hawaiian culture carried all the mana, the energy, and the male was the active principal. Without the feminine energy there would be no movement. So there is no creation or expression without the balance between the two.

WHAT DO I DO WITH MY THREE SELVES?

In the next chapter, we'll begin to explore how you create your personal universe and how to begin to work with your three selves. As with previous concepts, remember that learning about your three selves is about learning how to relate to who you are. Many of us attempt to control things like our emotions consciously. We think if we think happy thoughts, that everything will be okay. But having a PhD in psychology, I can assure you that long before positive thinking became popular and long before affirmations became trendy, psychology attempted to persuade us that conscious happy thoughts were the key to happy emotions.

According to the Western approach (which views the conscious mind as all powerful), we just need a little focus and determination to control our emotions. However, the emotions are a part of the unconscious mind. Haven't you been in the middle of a great day when, seemingly out of nowhere, sadness (or another negative emotion) leaps up to the surface? And when you tried to consciously control or dismiss that negative emotion, you simply couldn't shake it? That's because emotion does not belong to the realm of the conscious.

When you learn about the role of the unconscious, you realize that the unconscious is the aspect of you that is responsible for the release of emotions, not the conscious mind. When you learn the role of each mind, you learn what aspect (or mana) to call upon in a given situation. Should you think it through, trust the gut, or look for guidance from above? Each situation is different, and each of your selves (and sometimes all three) participates in the solution.

SUMMARY:

1. We have three selves or minds: conscious, unconscious and higher conscious.

2. The selves each relate to one of the bodies: conscious with the mental body, unconscious with the emotional body and higher conscious with the spiritual body.

3. The unconscious mind is the critical link between the conscious mind and higher conscious mind.

Formlessness

Keawe
Makes room for movement
(space)

AIR
movement

HOT   WET

FIRE   WATER

Expansion   Contraction

DRY   COLD

Stability, no movement

EARTH
Covers up the space
created by Keawe

CHAPTER FIVE: THE FIVE ELEMENTS

THE HAWAIIAN CREATION STORY: KUMULIPO

According to Leilani Melvil, a writer who has written one of many books on the creation chant Kumulipo (see also Martha Beckwith), once upon a time there was nothing and there was everything. But everything was contained in a single seed smaller than anything you could imagine. Infinitely small, yet infinitely large. There was no time and there was a deep nothingness called po. There was also Keawe, which is "essence" or "substance." Suddenly in one moment, the Keawe moved and a huge burst of energy and light came out of it. The entire universe was thus created.

This story has been told in Hawai'i since the time of the ancients. They had the big bang theory (or at least a chant that sounded a lot like the big bang theory) far earlier than Western physicists conceived it. Based on the translations of ancient chants, it's difficult to tell

whether they believed that flash of light actually created the four basic elements (the fifth element being Keawe itself). But I think that's how these elements came to be.

Quantum physicists say there was first the space between the space, the nothingness. Then came condensed light and raw energy. The light and energy combined and matter became manifest: atoms, subatomic atoms, quarks, neutrinos and so on to become coffee tables and bowling balls. At the deepest level, that original energy reaches all the way out into physical manifestation.

All of the elements in the Hawaiian creation story are said to come from the source, the Keawe. The first element created was the air element. The air element creates room for movement and is movement itself. As the air element moved, it created friction, which brought the creation of the fire element. The fire element is expansion. It's transformation; it's electric. The fire element created a condensation, which then gave birth to the water element. The water element is contraction and it is nurturing. All three of these elements – air, fire, and water – came together to create the fourth element, earth. Earth is stability, no movement, grounding, foundation.

Not Just Theoretical Knowledge

When I was in fourth grade, I decided I wanted to be a police officer, probably inspired by watching Hawai'i Five-O and Magnum PI. Those guys were the ultimate cool. They got to ride bicycles. They got to wear shorts. They had badges and guns. What more could a young guy in Hawai'i aspire to? So in my early 20's, I studied criminal justice. Eventually I had a moment of clarity, recognized that my core intention was wanting to help people, so I chose to follow a different path. (My mother said she breathed a sigh of relief that day and drank a bottle of champagne!)

But I learned a truth from my criminal justice studies that I still find relevant today: ignorance of the law is not a defense. This simple idea is built into the majority of the legal systems around the planet. Ignorance of the law is not a defense. That means we can't break a law and claim that we didn't know about it to avoid repercussions.

Huna operates on the same premise. The energy of the universe and the five elements have their own laws. To claim "But I didn't know" is not a defense. We always have an option. We can either learn the laws and learn how to apply them, or let the laws direct us and remain victims. We can claim ignorance of gravity but it won't stop us from landing on our backsides when we leap from tall buildings! As Jack Kornfield said, "You can't stop the waves, but you can learn to surf."

That's why it's important to learn about the basic energies, the five elements. If you want to have more control over your personal energy levels and your physical world, you need to learn about the elements. As you gain understanding and become more familiar with these energies, you'll be able to call them and direct them more clearly.

These energies are everywhere. Some physical manifestations or movements are created of only one element, like water in a glass. Obviously this is water, and primarily the water element. Living things are a combination of all the elements. Animals, living creatures, plants and human beings are made up of all of these elements in varying degrees. So we need to understand each element as it stands alone and also how it relates to the others. Huna suggests that your ultimate goal as an individual would be to have the four basic elements balanced or in harmony within you, to remove any imbalance and be able to direct whatever element you need given the specific circumstance.

THAT ENERGY STUFF ISN'T REAL!

I have actually heard people say that "energy is just New Age woo-woo stuff" in my trainings. I don't hear it as much now as I did ten or fifteen years ago, but I still get a few comments like this. So let me be clear: Quantum physics has proven that energy exists and that it is at the deepest level of almost everything. The ancients were right, we live in a world of energy. Over the centuries, we lost that knowledge. Science claimed that metaphysical energy did not exist because we could not measure it. Now we measure it, so it is scientifically accepted.

Yet people still say, "I don't see it and I don't feel it. I don't get it. I don't understand." And that is precisely why I teach Huna principles of energy. We didn't learn about energy in elementary school, so we need to learn about it now. We have, however, learned about the effects of energy. Does this advertisement sound familiar? 6-Hour Energy Drink, Guaranteed No Crash!!

A person in a recent training I conducted in Newport Beach California was pretty skeptical about energy, yet he was very clear about how it works. When I asked the group, "How many of you have awakened on a day knowing you had a million things to do, and yet found you had no energy to get going. What do you do?" "Grab an espresso!" the skeptic yelled. I said "Great, you're not sure about energy and the elements, but you're clear that when you don't have them, you need to eat or drink something." Next I asked about the opposite: "How many of you have awakened on a day off and wanted to sleep in, but you had so much energy, you couldn't stay still?" Our skeptic yelled, "Just grab some meds to knock you out!!" Everyone laughed, as did I. But the point is that whether we are believers or not, all of us intuitively know that energy exists because we experience the effects of energy—or its lack. Most of us have figured out coping mechanisms to deal with energy's ups and downs. Huna teaches you to be your own espresso, your own energy drink or your own calming moment. Knowledge is power, if you do something with it. The following concepts about energy and elements are meant to be applied in your life – not just debated on the theoretical level.

WHAT YOU NEED TO KNOW ABOUT THE ELEMENTS

When I first started teaching Huna, the very first course I was shown how to teach was about the elements because they are so important. They are the basic building blocks of all energy in the universe.

In order to work with these building blocks effectively, you need to grasp a few key concepts.

Hawaiian	English	Indian	Qualities	Sound	Color
Keawe	Space	Akasha	Spirit Void	Ham U	Purple Black
Makani Ha	Air	Vayu	Breath Sky	Yam A	Light Blue
Ahi	Fire	Tejias Agni	Light Heat	Ram Sh	Red Sunlight
Wai	Water	Apas	Cooling	Vam M	Deep Blue
Honua	Earth	Prithivi	Solid	Lam B	Yellow Brown Gray

First, knowing the name of each element is essential. In ancient times, you might not be given the name of the element until you reached a certain level. In this chapter, you will learn the Hawaiian name of the element. It is also critical that you learn how to pronounce each element. I've included phonetic spellings to guide you (or you can order the CD entitled "Working with the Elements" by visiting www.Huna.com or emailing info@huna.com). The Hawaiian name for each element carries energy in the very word itself. The Hawaiians believed breath was very important. Understanding the breath and the vibration of the word that represents each element will increase that element inside you.

Knowing the particular qualities of each element is another key. This is similar to getting to know another person where it's important to

understand their personality, likes and dislikes. It's always harder to work with total strangers than with folks you know well. The more intimately you get to know each element, the more easily you will be able to direct it. When you get to know each element, it becomes your friend.

Knowing the color associated with each element will also increase your ability to call the element and direct it. And finally, the symbol of the element is key. Many ancient traditions acknowledged these elements and had symbols associated with them. The symbols used in this Huna system are the ones in the chart below and were on the desk of Papa Bray as he taught my father our lineage of Huna.

The chart above shows the Hawaiian name, the English name, and the Eastern Indian name of each element. It gives a quick snapshot of the quality, color and the sound associated with each element. Under the sound column, you'll see the mantras from the Tantric tradition associated with each element. [1]

AIR: MAKANI (MAH KAHN EE)

Makani is the air element. It is also the word ha (pronounced "hah"), which is "breath." Makani is the breeze around you while ha is the breath that comes from inside you. Air is the element of movement. Ancient Hawaiians called the trade wind makani, the life-giving spirit of air. Makani rules the mental plane and it rules kilokilo (divination). The breath that is associated with the air element is the holding of the in-breath. You may have noticed that when you concentrate on something, like a crossword puzzle or something that requires your focus, you find yourself breathing in then holding your breath. This is a natural way in which the body works with the air element.

Huna says that physical manifestation is always preceded by the air element so makani is associated with creation. This means that before something comes to be, it starts as a thought. From spirit comes a spark or idea: "This is what I want to do. This is who I want to be." Before that thought even gets to the emotional or physical plane, it starts in the mental body which is ruled by air. Many practices in Huna involve ha breathing techniques. Ha breathing brings a focus of thought. When you breathe the word ha, you bring in or call in the air element.

The color for air is a light blue and its symbol is a pale, blue disk. Think of the color of a light blue sky with no clouds. The sound or mantra associated with the air element in Sanskrit is yam. In the body, air relates to the chest and lungs. Too much air, you can feel hungry, restless. Too little air, not so hungry.

FIRE: AHI (AH HEE)

In the Huna system, we are told that we have an imu (oven) in the pit of our stomachs. An imu is like a cauldron and the Hawaiians put it in the ground for cooking. Your imu is below your solar plexus, right below the belly button. Within the Chakra system, it would be just below the 3rd Chakra and it is the source of your mana (energy). Therefore, even though fire is mostly associated with the head in the Hawaiian system, they also relate your imu area to the fire element.

Ahi or fire is expansion. It is electric; it is the sun, heat and light. It is our expressiveness, aggressiveness and our passion. Ahi is the masculine or yang aspect. It is related to desire and rules digestion. Fire shakes up existing conditions to prepare us for change. It also provides the spark,

1 A note: We teach the Sanskrit mantras because different students may find a different way to closer connection. We learned a long time ago that the way one person experiences energy is different from another. Therefore, in our tradition, we provide as many ways possible to connect, while at the same time, we respect our lineage and the cultural information.

passion and desire to motivate you to take action. Some people flow this energy naturally and we describe them as people who "have a fire in their belly."

Too much fire can result in physical manifestations such as fever or indigestion. Not enough fire can result in a lack of passion or desire, an inability to get moving.

The colors for ahi are red and yellow and the symbol is an upward-facing red triangle. In the Hawaiian system, one of the raw sounds associated with the fire element was the sound of putting a hot frying pan into the cold water: shhh. This sound will help bring up some of the fire element.

WATER: WAI (VWAI)

The element of wai (water) represents contraction, shrinking, and nurturing. It is the moon, a magnetic force. Water is the feminine principle, yin, and it is our emotional nature. Water is typically associated with the middle of the body or the waist area. Though wai is spelled with a "w," it is pronounced with a slight "v" sound; rather than "why," you pronounce it like "vhy."

The water element is cooling. It's the moon, feminine energy, yin, magnetic. Wai is our emotional nature and it rules the emotional body. Although water is the nurturer, it also fluctuates or offers a feeling of fluctuation and movement.

The colors associated with water are deep ocean blue. Water changes color the farther you get from the land. Where the land mass drops down abruptly off the coast, the ocean reflects a deep blackish-blue, the color associated with the water element. The Hawaiian symbol for water is an upward-facing crescent moon. The symbol is the color of a silvery moon. So there are two colors associated with water; silver and the dark ocean blue.

With too much of the water element, you can literally have water retention in the physical body. When moving the energy of this element you may feel heavier, or that you've slowed down. You may feel more nurtured. You may feel calm or mellow. You might feel cooler or sense that you have more saliva in your mouth.

EARTH: HONUA (HOH NU AH)

Honua (earth) is said to be the sacred womb, the mother of all physical creation. It rules the physical plane and creates density and gravity. Earth is stability, support and strength. It is solidity itself, the combination of the other elements being produced by an interaction of fire, air, and water.

The earth element is one of the two balancing elements. If you have an excess of the other elements, the honua can offer balance. If you're not feeling grounded, the earth element can offer connection. If your head is in the clouds, or there's too much fire or emotion in your life, work with the earth element. This element can also assist in resolving physical pains related to a lack of support, like joints or muscles or connective tissues because the earth element rules the physical plane. Becoming a really good director of the earth element puts you in charge of the energy that rules your physical body.

The color associated with the earth element is a yellow, brownish color, like the soil, or a gray like the gray of an old rock. The symbol for earth is a yellow or brownish square. In the physical body, earth is usually associated with legs and feet

KEAWE: ETHER, SPACE (KAY AH VWAY)

Fire, water, air and earth relate to and interact with each other. In many systems, there are only these four elements. In order to be classified as an element in these systems, it had to be a raw, metaphysical energy that can be contained. But Keawe is different. It is in everything, and it is the space that is between us. In other systems, Keawe[2] is referred to as Source. These systems would say, "You cannot contain the Keawe. The Keawe is. The Keawe is not. The Keawe is everywhere, and the Keawe is nowhere."

---

2 There were some native Hawaiians whose lineage linked directly to Keawe. These people worked directly with Keawe and wouldn't even mention the private name but used the more public name Keawe. I do not mention these other names in this book because they are felt to be private and sacred, similar to the special name that you call your partner only in private. When these names were taught to my father, it was also emphasized that the public names should be used except in specific circumstances.

The Hawaiian system took a different approach and chose to group Keawe with the other elements. At the same time, the system recognized that Keawe did not act like the other elements. Still, Huna refers to it as an element because you can draw it in, you can build it up inside you, and you can flow it around a room. However, they also recognized that it is uncontainable and outside the realm of the other elements and therefore, more an essence of spirit in nature.

Keawe is the spirit space, the space between the space in all existence that has been identified by quantum physics, the nothingness. One of the first published works on quantum physics I ever read discussed the fact that a table is mostly made up of empty space. Quantum physics dug a bit deeper to find that between the nucleus of an atom and the subatomic particle circling it, there is immense space. If you blew the nucleus up to the size of a building the subatomic particle would be miles away. As physicists delved even deeper into the quantum, they found even smaller items such as quarks and neutrinos.

Next they found a level of raw energy, which I find interesting because almost every ancient culture knew about energy. As physicists became able to measure more deeply than the energy level, they found condensed light. Interesting as well because most ancient cultures explained that we are beings of light, and now science reaffirms that notion! When scientists delved even deeper than condensed light, they found a second layer of space, which is the space between the space. One quantum physicist wrote that they found the resting place of God, because all ancient scriptures point to the fact that the higher self, Keawe, God, rests at the space between the space.

So Keawe is a unifying element that lies beyond physical consciousness. This element makes room for movement to occur. You can build up a lot of Keawe but as soon as you stop focusing on it, it instantly disperses. It goes back into the universe, and unlike other elements, Keawe cannot be contained.

As Uncle George explained, it seemed on the surface that Hawaiians worshiped many gods. However, it was known that all the gods flowed from one Source, the Keawe. Since you could not direct the Keawe you had to work with a manifestation or intermediaries to communicate with Keawe. For instance, if you lived near Kilauea Volcano, you talked to Pele, the goddess of fire, to get a message to the Keawe. You used Pele because Pele was your next-door neighbor and had the direct connection to Keawe. So you talk to Pele, Pele talks to Keawe, and everything is handled. Yet even though you usually used an intermediary, to ignore and not know about Keawe would be to ignore the Source where everything originates.

Keawe is the element of pure cause and effect, which makes it the vehicle for sending thought forms. If you are gifted at perceiving what someone else is thinking or sending mental messages to others, you are probably naturally gifted at working with the Keawe. Keawe also implies truthfulness and honesty and it is the trance element. It is the destination when dropping into the void. During meditation, if you've ever suddenly felt like you've disappeared and that your body has transcended for a moment, that's when you've dropped into the void, the Keawe inside. It lies beyond physical consciousness and you lose the ability for cognitive thinking. You might stop breathing when you drop into the void and return to conscious state with the gasp of air.

Like earth, Keawe is a balancing element, a unifying element. If you feel that your elements are out of balance, you can draw upon or focus on the Keawe to balance all the elements inside you.

Archetypically, the spirit element is purple, and in the Hawaiian system the color is a purple or a dark, blackish purple. The symbol for Keawe is a purplish black upward facing oval.

WHAT AM I SUPPOSED TO DO WITH ENERGY?

In addition to what we will be covering in the rest of the book, it is important to realize what gives you energy in general (helps you build it up) and what takes away your energy. I used to be a bit heavier, and I inhaled Haagen-Dazs

Chocolate Chip Cookie Dough by the pint! As I'd start a new pint, I'd have a little discussion with myself: "Why am I eating this?" "Just one more bite!" "Oh, I can't leave a little in the pint. I better just finish it!" Then the finale was, of course, "Wow, I feel awful."

That last part of the internal conversation is an important acknowledgement. Eating certain foods, doing certain activities, or thinking certain thoughts will decrease your energy. Other foods, activities or thoughts will increase your energy. Pay attention to the simplest variations of energy caused by your actions, thoughts and foods. Soon, you will be able to feel and work with the five energies in your environment.

SUMMARY:

1. The five elements or energies are the building blocks of everything in the universe.

2. Each element has its own characteristics and works according to its own laws.

3. By becoming familiar with these elements, we can direct them and balance them within ourselves and our environments.

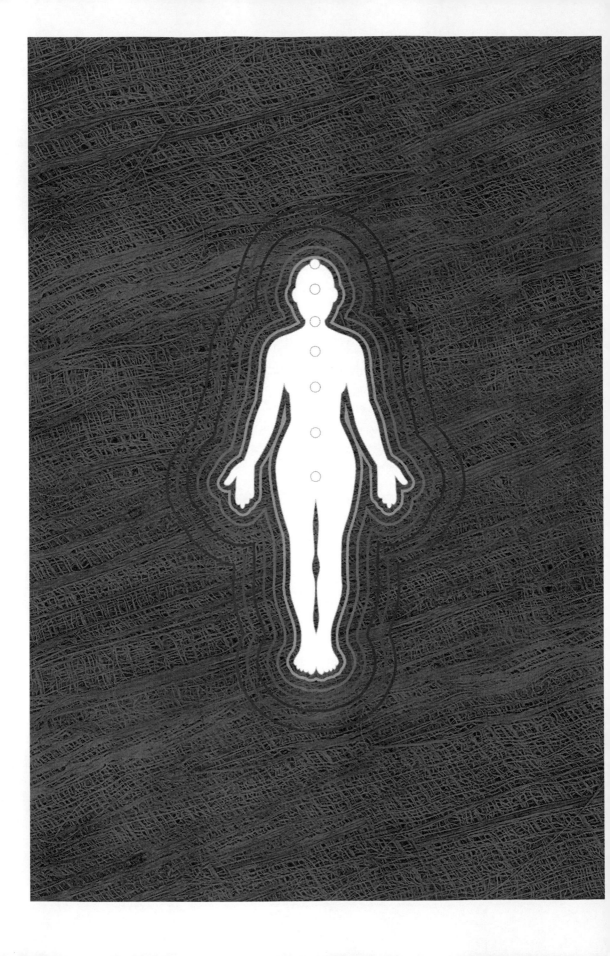

Chapter Six: Working with the Energies

The basic universal elements in the previous chapter are the basic building blocks of everything around us. In ancient times people viewed all things as energy: the chair, drum, wall – all was seen as metaphysical energy. But as Western scientific thinking developed, it basically claimed, "If we can't see it or prove it, it doesn't exist." The original scientists and alchemists took objects like a piece of wood and broke them down to their smallest components. They couldn't see any energy so they determined that there was none.

The objective scientific model moved most of us away from the concept that all things are energy at the deepest level. The ancient people who could tell you what earth, fire, water or air elements an object contained either disappeared or went underground. We eventually got to a point where we completely forgot the old teachings, especially in Western societies. We became separate from our universe. We could observe ourselves and our environment but came to believe that we had no effect on them whatsoever.

Fortunately, science is transforming. Quantum physicists dug deeper and deeper to get past the atoms into the quantum. They revealed smaller and smaller particles and the constant movement of these particles. They discovered the space between the space, the resting place of Keawe. At the deepest level of the quantum, they discovered that all matter is made up of light and raw energy. And though they've not yet created instruments sophisticated enough to make the distinction, what exactly is raw energy? It is the four elements as taught by Papa Bray to my father: air, fire, water and earth.

Recent research indicates that this raw energy may be made up of different frequencies. My belief is that some day soon, they will classify the raw energy as four different frequencies similarly to frequencies of brain wave patterns.

Technically, we don't have four distinct brain waves. Rather, we have brain waves that fall into one of four measurable frequencies. Raw energy is similar. As some quantum physicists admit, we have come full circle back to the wisdom of the ancient teachings.

The ancients used the words air, fire, water and earth not because those physical things resided in you, but rather because raw energy could be felt in different ways. For example, we have all felt so much passion about something that we begin to get "fired up" about the topic. The ancients felt the qualities of the various forms of raw mana, then used common, relatable words for substances with similar qualities in their environment. Very practical. Why invent a new word? These common labels helped with understanding.

THREE TYPES OF MANA (ENERGY)

In Huna, not all energy is the same and there are three levels of higher energies or vibrations. (Quantum physicists haven't found this yet. We're waiting for them to catch up!) Those levels of energies have different qualities and each of them have the potential to direct the others. They interact with one another other yet each is within the basic domain of one of the three selves.

The first type of mana is basic life-force energy. It runs the various processes in the body and is in the domain of the unconscious mind.

According to the Bray family lineage of Huna, the next classification of energy is manamana. In Hawaiian, a word that is put together twice creates a greater emphasis. It increases the word's value, intensity, or purpose. So manamana is a more intense energy. Manamana is the domain of the conscious mind. It is the energy that allows you to control your conscious mind and direct it. Have you ever become so focused on a task that you felt a surge of energy in your body? That's manamana.

The third or highest level of vibration or energy is manaloa, which is in the domain of the higher self. As manaloa comes in, its energy has a cleansing, healing quality. Manaloa naturally makes it easier for you to release negative emotions. It naturally clears out obstacles, and it clears out or releases attachments and fixations. The manaloa can also align the three selves, the four bodies, and assist you in releasing any conflicts. When you have that spiritual experience where you feel that all is right with the world, you are experiencing manaloa energy.

Where the elements represent a type of energy, mana, manamana, and manaloa represent the level of its vibration. So you can have mana that is fire or manaloa that is fire. The situation determines which you access.

HA BREATHING

Ha is breath. In Huna as well as in most traditional systems throughout the planet, the breath is incredibly important. Before I chant,

Etua taught me to do ha breathing. Before I meditate, I was instructed to do ha breathing. Uncle George once told me that the ancient Kahuna actually would get together in groups and do ha breathing for days, working in shifts to build up the mana or the energy needed for a large undertaking.

Ha breathing is simple but powerful. You inhale through your nose and exhale out your mouth. The relationship between the inhale to the exhale is a one to two relationship. In other words, you inhale through your nose to the count of two or four and exhale through your mouth to a count of four or eight, always using a one to two relationship between inhale and exhale. As you exhale, you make the soft sound "Haaaaaaa."

I once asked Uncle George, "Why is the ha, the breath, so important to the Hawaiians?" He explained, "The breath is the basis of life. If you want to learn how to control anything – energy, higher self, mana, your thoughts – you've got to start with the breath because the breath gives you life. If you can't control your breath, how can you expect to control the most powerful universal energy around you?"

The ha sound in the exhale is gentle. And the ha is prolonged. You don't let the whole ha out in the beginning. You maintain a consistent release, as best you can, for about a count of four. You may wish to stand with your feet just beyond shoulder width and extend your hands outward to the right and left with palms facing up. If your arms get tired you can breathe with them in by your side.

When we do ha breathing, we are actually working with two elements. One of them is air because of the vibration of the sound. The second is water because we're lengthening our breath. The lengthening of the breath on the exhale (in comparison to the inhale) is calling in the water element. So essentially, the ha breath brings in air and water.

You may find that you eyes water up while doing ha breathing. This is because it brings in an emotional quality to it and it brings in the water element. Air and water are very positive for meditating as they create a calm, centered and balanced state that brings focus and clarity.

SOURCE OF YOUR ENERGY

In Ho'omana, the Huna system, the goal is to be in charge of your energy, not at the mercy of it. Regardless of what has occurred, you can bring in whatever mana you need because the universe and you have an infinite source of energy.

During an energy seminar in a different discipline that I took as a young adult, the instructor talked about flowing energy and the abundance of energy in the universe. He said that the universe has an unlimited supply of energy that you can tap into at anytime. I remember thinking, "This is good news. We're not going to run out. We have lots of energy and that's really good."

But then the instructor said "Make sure that you always flow energy from outside yourself. Because if you flow energy from within, you can deplete it all and you can die." This definitely was not good news. I got really nervous for a second and wrote in my notebook, "Always flow energy from outside because you only have a limited supply inside, and if you run out your gas tank goes empty and the car stops!"

Fortunately, shortly thereafter, I remembered some Huna teachings from Papa Bray and from Uncle George on the subject of energy flow. If the universe has an unlimited amount of energy and "as above, is so below" is true, who else has an unlimited amount of energy? We all do! That was really good news!

After discussing the apparent dichotomy with my father, I realized that I could respect my seminar teacher for his beliefs – but it was his reality, not mine. Here's my reality: Whether you flow energy from outside through you or whether you flow it from inside out, it's still the same thing. One of the assumptions of Huna and physics is that nature abhors a vacuum. If you create an empty space, nature wants to fill it. So even if you did flow all of the energy inside your body, the universe would just naturally want to fill you back up again.

FLOWING THE ENERGY

When the concept of energy is presented in workshops, it seems like it is something esoteric or "woo woo." But in our daily lives, we talk about energy all the time. We wake up some mornings feeling like we "just don't have enough energy" to deal with the activities of the day before us. We feel "energized" by upbeat music, fun interactions or exciting ideas. We face an unpleasant or complex situation and may realize that we "don't have the energy to deal with it." We look at someone who is particularly productive and upbeat and describe him or her as having "a lot of energy."

Beyond quantifying energy, we are also very good at making distinctions in types of energy. You may not be paying much conscious attention to it, but you constantly sense and react to different energies in your daily life. Think about hugs for example. When someone hugs you, can't you feel the energy behind it? It may feel full, warm and loving or it may feel tight, distant and cold. It may include a hint of desperation, a sense of relief, or a flavor of nurturing. Some hugs may feel lustful or sexual (a distinction that women tend to notice more than men!). The physical movement of the hugs themselves may be very similar in all cases, but we are naturally aware of their different energies or intentions. And when we hug someone and wish to express a particular emotion or intention, we don't have to give a lot of thought to flowing that energy. We don't need instruction; we do it naturally.

Eventually you'll have done so much work with the elements that it will feel as natural as the different hugs you offer. It will be like going into the gym. You know what weight to pick up, how to do the exercise and when to go on to the next one. After a while, you'll be able to call the elements easily, and move and flow them.

SENSING THE ENERGY

In the Huna workshops, I use various exercises to help students tune into energy. One is a partnered exercise where each student stands face to face with another person. Both partners extend arms in front and have their palms about two inches from their partner's palms. Energy will flow from their right palms and be received by their left palms, forming a circuit. I ask them to relax and focus attention on the sensations in their palms. As the partners imagine flowing and receiving energy, they allow their palms and arms to move broad circular motions, feeling the energy circulate between them. As they do this, I ask them to describe the energy to themselves: What are its qualities? How does it feel? After a time, we switch partners to allow them to feel the energy of a new partner.[1]

ENERGY OF THE ELEMENTS

Becoming familiar with the energy of the elements is similar to feeling and becoming familiar with another person's energy. In the Huna workshops, we have several exercises to do this. But here are some you can do on your own:

---

1 A note: it is best to do this exercise with a partner who is not very familiar to you. When you know someone really well, unconsciously you also know their energy. Unconsciously, it may be so familiar to you, like their scent or their pattern of speech, that you have a hard time feeling the energy consciously.

Air: Stand outside on a breezy day. Allow yourself to feel relaxed yet focused as when doing the partnered exercise. Feel the breeze and its qualities of movement, possibility and coolness, and visualize its light blue color. Imagine the air energy flowing into you through your back. Now imagine that same energy flowing from you, out through your palms then circling up and back to rejoin the air coming in. Use the ha breathing described on page 69: receive the air energy as you inhale and flow it outward as you exhale slowly making the sound "haaa."

Fire: Stand before a fire, or you can use any source of heat and imagine it to be a fire. Feel the fire and its qualities of electricity, masculinity and passion, and visualize its bright yellow and red color. Imagine that energy flowing into you and allow it to flow back out through your palms. You can use a modified version of the ha breathing: Inhale slowly to the count of four and receive the fire energy. Exhale more quickly to the count of two making the sound "shhhh."

Water: If you are lucky enough to live near a beach, that's a wonderful place to get in touch with the water element and its energy. Walk into the water and feel the movement of the waves. But if that's not possible, standing in a gentle rain or even in your shower will do the trick. As with the partnered exercise and those of the other elements, allow yourself to feel relaxed yet focused. Allow yourself to feel the water's qualities: nurturing, feminine, magnetic. Imagine its deep blue color. Imagine that energy flowing into you and out through the palms of your hands. Since the ha breath is the air and water element, you may use it here too. Instead of the sound "ha," just exhale with a gentle sound of "mmmmmmmm," a nurturing low rumbling sound.

Earth: Because of its solidity, earth is often the easiest element for many of us experience. Stand outside in your bare feet. Feel the stability, the support, the strength of the earth beneath your feet and allow those qualities to come up into your body. Visualize the yellow brown color of the earth and let the earth energy flow back outward through your hands. When working with the earth element, just keep all your breathing even and focused.

Keawe: In the Huna training, we delve more deeply into working with Keawe than the scope of this book will allow. But to give you a sense of the aumakua energy available to you, sit quietly and do the ha breathing (page 69) for 5 to 10 minutes. As you do so, focus on the area of your lower belly, your gut. When you feel completely relaxed and centered, gently call to aumakua: "Dear aumakua, please float above me." Continue your breathing and allow whatever happens next to happen. You may have an insight or a vision. You may simply feel a sense of well being. Do not judge or worry about the experience. Accept whatever aumakua offers you.

INDIVIDUAL EXPERIENCE

What we experience when we work with energy will be different for each of us. If you feel the energy and experience it as hot, that's neither right or wrong. It's perfect for you. If your neighbor feels that same energy as cold, that is perfect as well. Everyone will feel the energy differently and everyone will have a different experience while flowing the energy. When you're flowing one of the elements to someone else, they may experience it differently than you do. Fire may feel cool, tingly, or hot. A variety of factors plays into our experience.

For example, when I first became involved with Huna, I had an imbalance of fire. I was just naturally a very fiery person. During a training, I did energy flow work with another participant. He said "Wow, my hand's hot! Do you feel the heat?" But the energy coming from his hands felt cool to me. I had so much fire that his fire actually seemed cool to me in comparison. Remember, there's no right or wrong in how you experience the energies.

Some of us will feel tired after a session of flowing energy and others will feel revitalized. If you generally feel tired afterward, it doesn't matter if you focus on using the energy inside or outside. You'll probably still feel tired. If you typically feel energized, you'll feel energized.

It's like starting an exercise program. Some people will go into the gym and feel energized while others will feel tired for a week or so. It doesn't matter. The longest I've ever seen it take to bring the body back into balance from energy work is about three days, and that particular person was doing some very intense energy workouts. Usually a good night's rest, eating a nice meal and drinking some water brings the body back into balance fairly quickly.

The energy will take care of filling you back up. Wherever it comes from, whether it's from inside or outside, just direct it. Give your concentration to the energy and the flow of that energy, and the energy will take care of the rest. As above, so below.

The Five Elements

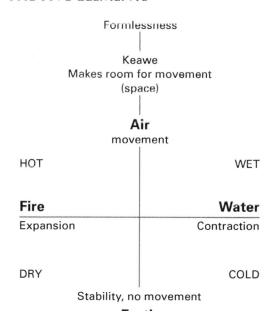

Formlessness
|
Keawe
Makes room for movement
(space)
|

Air
movement

HOT | WET

Fire | **Water**
Expansion | Contraction

DRY | COLD

Stability, no movement
Earth
Covers up the space
created by Keawe

Balancing Act

When any element makes you feel out of balance, it could be one that you haven't experienced a lot. You may need to work with it or you may need to balance it by calling on another element. The diagram above tells you what elements provide balance and which are opposites. In Huna, the elements of fire and water are opposite to one another, as are air and earth. Air and earth are the mediators between water and fire. Water and fire are the mediators between air and earth. As we seek to balance the energies or elements within ourselves, it's usually not appropriate to use an element's opposite. Instead, you use a mediator.

For example, if a person has too much fire element (passion or anger), you don't want to add more water (emotion, fluctuation) to the situation. Fire is the sun, water is the moon; fire is electric, water is magnetic. Think of what happens when you throw a hot frying pan into cold water– the result is almost explosive! Instead of water, you may want to bring in a balancing element, perhaps some air to cool the fire or some earth to ground the fire. When your hand is wet, you don't find fire to dry it off. Either you blow on it (use of makani) or you take something dry and wipe your hand dry (like honua).

Another example: You get very hot (fire) which makes you sweat (water). What do you do to dry yourself? Typically, you take off your coat, fan yourself or open a window (introduce more air). When there's too much of the physical water element, we bring in the balancing element of air. We don't jump in a fire to dry off! Many of the things that Huna teaches about the elements are reflected in our everyday, common activities. In a sense, Huna does not explain anything new, rather it teaches you to be conscious of what is natural for you.

Have you ever been around someone who has trouble getting motivated? The common saying is that we want to "light a fire under them." When someone gets stuck, they have an imbalance of the earthbound element. No amount of air is going to get new thoughts in. You've got to light a fire, get some movement going, get some expansion occurring.

The elements are a natural part of our language and hard-wired into our neurology. It's been in our language for centuries because of teachings in the past. You may have heard the expression that an unfocused person has "his head in the clouds." That's basically saying that he or she is out of balance and needs the grounding earth element to get stabilized.

If your emotions are erratic, you might bring in some of the water element to begin to get into balance. If you want to slow down or if you want to get in touch with the way you feel about something, the water element is very positive. If you've gone through something traumatic or emotionally depleting, you may want to move the water element and nurture yourself.

PERMISSION TO FLOW ENERGY TO OTHERS

I'm a firm believer in working with permission. Imagine if you had a coworker who said, "I'm not feeling very much passion right now," and you spontaneously let out a "sh, haaaa" breath. Your desire to help is commendable but you didn't have permission from that person to do it.

Not only do you run the risk of freaking someone out, your efforts would be in vain if they were skeptical or not really ready!

Most of us intuitively know when we have permission from another person. You consult the little Jiminy Cricket in your head and you just know. But if you check with Jiminy and you still aren't sure, just ask the other person. You'll be amazed at how many people are interested in quantum physics, energy and spirituality. In Hawai'i, we say that there's no reason to be ashamed of what it is that you know. We have no problem saying, "Hey, I know a little bit about energy. Can I put my hands over your shoulders and flow you some positive energy?" In fact you've probably had someone say something similar to you asking if they can send you some positive energy, some positive thoughts, a prayer. That's permission.

Get to know each element and when to use it. Get to know how this element interacts with you and the situations where it is appropriate.

THE ENERGY OF PRAYER

After many years studying psychology, I can tell you without a doubt, that energy and spirituality have been omitted from most of Western thinking. That we have energy in our life as well as the ability to master it has been viewed as irrational, "new age" or "woo-woo." (When I was looking for a dissertation topic for my PhD in psychology, I was thrilled to hear the dean of the department mention that "there aren't enough dissertations coming through about spirituality." Music to my ears!)

One of my teachers (who became the Chairperson for my dissertation) was intrigued with the concepts of forgiveness and spirituality. After the tragedy of September 11th, she sent out a survey about how people were coping with the experience for an article she was writing. She specifically targeted non-New Yorkers to determine what the rest of the country was doing to cope. Her survey had a few prompts for various reactions and coping mechanisms, such as "donate money," "send a card to a survivor," or "visit New York to help tourism." Her final question was an open-ended blank for answers that didn't fit the suggestions. The number one response in that open-ended question was prayer. "I'm praying for them."

When she submitted the article to the journal contracting her piece, they said "We will not publish it unless you remove the entire section about the statistics related to prayer because it has nothing to do with psychology." Her response was firm. "We're not going to change our article. Either you'll publish it or I'll submit it somewhere else. We didn't go looking for prayer. It was offered by the survey participants. You can't keep ignoring the psychology of spirituality."

Many studies, like the 9/11 one, show how spirituality helps with coping. Prayer keeps your consciousness calm, centered and balanced. There's power in simply understanding that prayer can help, not to mention the benefits of intentionally tapping into prayer's power.

In many ways, the idea of having access to this power, this mana has been wiped out of our thinking and removed from what we learned as children. When you understand the concept of a higher conscious, you are empowered in and of yourself. When you take it away, it is more difficult for you to find true empowerment. You only know two-thirds of who and what you are. The Huna system says that you don't know yourself if you don't understand your higher conscious mind. And therefore, how could you ever become empowered?

In Huna, pule or prayer is a bit different than Western concepts of entreaties to an all powerful God. It is more akin to intimate discussions with the energies around you, or a discussion with someone about something. Pule is another of those Hawaiian words that doesn't translate well into English. According to John Ka'imikaua, pule is a form of prayer, but not as we know it.

Pule means to call or to ask for something. You can pule to your higher self, a tree, the water or to God as in a prayer. John Ka'imikaua emphasized the importance of pule in almost every aspect of life. He said that because many see it as being identical to prayer, they have left it out of practice. However, he emphasized that pule was for bringing in information and guidance from above. Since above could mean higher self, God, or just the collective, a pule helps to guide you in the direction you need.

The ancient religion of the Hawaiians was separate from Huna. When Queen Ka'ahumanu and King Kamehameha II abolished the kapu system (the system of rules and taboos that governed the kingdom), the religion or religious practice ended. The Hawaiians believed in gods and goddesses, yet they didn't worship multiple gods and goddesses as pagan religions do. They believed that everything came from one Source. Uncle George talked about this Source, and Papa Bray called it Keawe, one Source. But they believed that you couldn't know that Source directly. You needed an intermediary. So if you lived at the volcano, you prayed to Pele, the "volcano" to take your message to Source, similarly to the way that you pray to a saint to get your message to God in some religions.

It didn't matter to whom or what you prayed. Pule was the acknowledgment that "I'm a channel. I'm a conduit so I pule to call the energy I need to me." My kumu hula (teacher of hula)

Etua hates flying. Every time he gets on an airplane he says "Akua lele, please get me there safely." Akua means "god" and lele means "wind." I once had the audacity to say, "Etua, I've studied the Hawaiian gods and goddesses and I don't remember akua lele." He snapped back, "Oh, hush! I need to ask the wind for help." That's when I realized that pule isn't praying to Source in the sense of Christian prayer. It's more about realizing your connection to everything and calling on the energies for cooperation.

HOW TO BEGIN WORKING WITH THE ELEMENTS?

To begin, practice the breath work, pay attention to any imbalance in the energies you feel, and ask for guidance from your higher consciousness. When doing the breath work, pick an element that is not as comfortable for you. Practice connecting with it and using your breath to bring it in. This will help to establish balance. Also, begin to recognize when there is imbalance, and ask yourself, "Which element will balance this feeling?" We all know how to do this intrinsically. With just the focus of thought, you will feel a difference. The saying is that "energy flows where attention goes," so give this some attention.

Finally, check for guidance from above. Please do remember that from above should fit into your belief system. If that is God, great. If it is Higher Self, wonderful. Whatever it is for you by whatever name you call it, it is perfect for you. By taking the time to make sure you are pono consciously and unconsciously with aumakua, you will find that you are more balanced in life.

SUMMARY:

1. We are meant to work with the energies, the elements – not to be at their mercy.

2. Breath is the foundation for calling and flowing the energies.

3. To balance an element, use a mediator, not its opposite.

Chapter Seven: Basis of Reality

One of the basic concepts in Huna is that "perception is projection." This simple statement has a few layers of meaning. It's great to understand it in theory. But it will only enhance your life if you grasp it experientially.

You See What You Believe

On one level, perception is projection means that what you perceive as reality is based on the beliefs of your conscious and unconscious minds. You see what you believe to be true. You see what you expect to see. You interpret input based on your internal attitudes, prejudices, and personality.

Why don't we see objectively? For one thing, we simply get too much input to process it all. According to the book Flow by Mihaly Csikszentmihalyi, we are each surrounded by about two million bits of information per second at any given time. Our nervous systems can only process about 126 bits of information per second. So

out of the two million, our brain grabs 126 bits to process. To pare the data down to 126 bits, our brain ignores, distorts and/or generalizes the input. It makes sense that our brain would choose to process the 126 bits that seem familiar, true, and congruent with what it's already processing, right? With so much data to handle, why would our brains choose bits of data that are strange to it or at odds with what it believes to be true?[1]

_____

1 This always brings up the point, "What happens to the other 1, 999, 874 bits of data?" My father liked the metaphor of toothpicks. Imagine that there are two million toothpicks dropping at your feet every second. And every second, you reach down and grab 126 of them to bring into your nervous system. How quickly before the toothpicks are piled up above your head? Pretty quickly. That ever-growing pile of toothpicks represents how much information you do not see. Clearly, we perceive far less than what is actually happening!

So if a person's brain is hard-wired with the belief that "money doesn't grow on trees," that brain will pick up the 126 bits of data to support the idea that it's hard to earn a living and ignore the rest of the data. If another person is thoroughly convinced that cash is easy to come by – truly believes this to be true, not just hopes that it is true – he or she will see and experience only input that supports abundance and ease. The two people and their brains live in the same world, maybe with very similar circumstances. But the reality they perceive is totally different.

Now that same two million bits of information per second that are presented to me, are presented to you, are presented to the successful people and unsuccessful people, the happy people and the grouches. This is why in any given economic situation, you are able to find some people who are thriving and others who are barely surviving. Guess who's in charge of deciding which bits we grab? We are, you and me, both consciously and unconsciously. There is only so much you see and experience. It's totally up to you to choose your 126 bits. Switching from un-empowered to empowered is thus a process of finding the most life-enhancing 126 bits.

And as you choose and grab your 126 bits, you must remember that everything in the universe, including you, is so much more than what you have chosen. If you perceive that there is much sorrow in the world, there is. And there is more than that. If you consider yourself to be non-athletic, that's true. But you are more than that. We can get locked into our labels, attached to our 126 bits. We label ourselves as a wife or husband, a carpenter, a teacher, a CEO. But you can always grab a different 126 bits. At any given moment, you can be so much more than who you think you are. It's all out there, and yet it's all being projected from inside yourself.

Carl Jung loved the concept of perception is projection. He would say, "That's probably the thing that you need to learn the most of, and you're probably repeating this as a cycle in your life."

No Monopoly on Reality

Based on the concept of perception is projection, it's pretty obvious that reality is relative to the observer. Every being lives and creates a unique universe which can never be 100% identical to the reality of another. We all may experience our reality as the center of the universe. But it isn't.

Understanding that each of us has a unique reality was a powerful learning for me. It's sometimes mind-blowing to realize that everyone that we meet has his or her own reality. It's pointless to argue with someone about whether or not that reality is real. Huna is not about what path or reality is right or wrong. It teaches us to become more congruent in what we believe is real, and to keep in mind that there's more reality than what we perceive right now.

I have to admit that during the early part of my training career, I believed that there was one perception and one way of viewing things. Since then, I've noticed that this is an easy trap for teachers to fall into. They look outside themselves, trying to make sense of the world, and strive to come to a rational understanding. Freud was a classic example. Freud created his theories based on limited observations of certain patients and colored by the culture of his time. He generalized what he saw and determined that "Everyone must be like this."

I also fell into this trap related to the Huna I teach. In the beginning, I was certain that the Huna system was the "right" path. (I was correct in a sense; Huna was the right path for me but not necessarily for the entire world!) When I ran across students who experienced things outside of my realm of reality, I thought, "That's not possible. That's a cause and effect violation." But I woke up during one such interaction and realized, "That student is actually experiencing this. It is real for him."

While there are agreed-upon aspects of our reality, for example, "There is a floor," how you experience that floor is unique to you. Do you like it? Is it pretty? Do you enjoy walking on it? Your perception of the reality of the floor is unique to you. On the other hand, when you say "I am angry at my friend," that feeling and experience is almost entirely your own, "in your head." This is important from a Huna perspective, because if something is entirely

in your head, what does that mean? It means you can change your reality. Huna teaches that every aspect of reality from the floor to your emotions exists at least partially in your mind. Therefore, if you learn to be in control of your mind (higher, conscious, and unconscious), you are in control of your reality.

YOU AND NOT YOU

Quantum physics also speaks to the idea of perception is projection. It says that you can only see outside yourself and everything you see is you. Michael Talbot explains this well in his book, The Holographic Universe. He says that for many years we held the belief that we are separate from our universe and that we can observe it without being connected to it. This is called the observer effect and it says that our entire experience (sight, sound, feeling, smell, and taste) occurs in our mind, that we experience our reality in our heads. This concept says that rather than experiencing the external, we perceive it internally and then project it back out onto the world.

In some way, shape, or form the world is a projection of who and what you are. The world is a reflection of you, so there's good news and bad news. The good news is that it's a reflection of you. The bad news is that it's a reflection of you. But the bottom line is that there really isn't anything that is not you.

Looking at the world in this way takes practice. I will still occasionally look at someone and think of them as "that person." As soon as I think that thought, I've not only separated myself from the other person but I've disconnected from all things. I've fooled myself into thinking "that person" is not me, and "that person" and his actions have "caused" something to happen in my life. Haven't we all been there? It's "that guy's" fault, not mine. You've just moved to the effect side of the equation.

When I was a kid, my grandfather would say, "Anytime you point at someone, you have three fingers pointing back at you." He was trying to remind me that I probably have a lot more to do with what happened in my life than I wanted to believe. Taking it one step further, when you point at someone else, you are really pointing at yourself. "That person," "that group of people," "that object" are all really you. As Carl Jung once said, "Projections change the world into the replica of one's own unknown face."

From a Huna perspective, when you feel this separation, the point is to ask yourself, "What is the learning that I need in order to realize that person is me?" For instance, if you spent most of your life in the water element, you might be put off when first meeting a person with a fiery personality. "That person" might look very aggressive to you. But if she is really you, what are you to learn? Rather than judging "that person" as bad, perhaps it is to recognize that she has an abundance of fire. Is the fire element calling to you? Could you use more fire in your life or a better understanding of it?

It's not only about looking at the seemingly negative aspects of others. You are also a mirror reflection of all that is beautiful and right in the world. Have you ever seen someone who is skilled or talented and thought, "I wish I could do that?" If you can see it, that ability is inside of you. You just need to learn how to own it, express it. Huna teaches that when you look at the world and see something you want to experience, have or be, those things are already you. You are projecting that desire out from the inside.

Etua teaches Hula to a group of 40 to 50 people at our Huna trainings. He often tells them, "When I look out at you, all I can see is a mirror reflection of me. I see you each as individuals and I know all I'm seeing is myself back. So by the end of the week when I've taught you the dance, what you dance is what I've taught you, and that's me, yet it's you."

AS ABOVE, SO BELOW

Hermes Trismegistus, pen name for the ancient Greeks who authored the Emerald Tablet, states in the Law of Correspondence "that which is above is like that which is below."

"Bring down that which is above by the means of the light, to ascend and take from darkness into the light that which is below by means of the light. This will transform the spiritual energy as it flows from the source and integrates all the islands." Kapihe, Kahuna, 1850 in Kona.

It's another way of saying perception is projection: E iho ana o luna, E pi'i ana o lalo. Lalo means "the below" and luna means "the above." What is above is like that which is below, and that which is below is like that which is above. In Huna, everything in your consciousness is considered "below" and the external world extending outside of your consciousness is "above."

In our personal evolution, initially we typically think that reality is outside of us. It is merely the objective "what is" and we have no part in its creation. Later, many of us hit the stage where we recognize that we have a personal reality. We might come to the point where we think that all reality is merely subjective, that it's entirely in our head. Many teachings stop there.

But Huna takes it one step further. Yes, your personal reality is a product of your conscious and unconscious beliefs and hard-wiring. But there is a reality that exists beyond or despite your mind's machinations. The grass and the concrete road exist whether you choose to include them in your 126 bits or not. I may think concrete is beautiful and you may perceive it as ugly, but basically we'll agree that it is pretty hard, strong stuff. Neither of us will win the beautiful versus ugly debate (a product of the below). But it's not too difficult to come to agreement about concrete's "above" nature: hard and strong.

The interesting thing is the relationship between the two. We can't just focus on what is below (internal) and ignore what is above (external). This is where students of the Law of Attraction are often frustrated. Holding a positive outlook internally while trying to ignore harsher circumstance externally doesn't seem to cut it.

On the other hand, we lose all of our power when we assume that there is nothing but the external reality of the above. Our imaginations have always allowed us to see what is possible before it takes form. Our desires draw us to seek more and to expand our reality. Many believe that life is about suffering and that things are hard. However, Huna teaches that the natural state of being is that of pono and positive. Therefore, when something doesn't feel good or positive, it is feedback from one or both sides of your reality that there is more to learn and become aware of.

BOTH REALITIES

My family was very involved with the Siddha Yoga Foundation. One summer as a child, I was allowed to ride around in a limousine with Baba Muktananda, the Indian swami who brought siddha yogic teachings to the West, and his translator. It was one of my first experiences connecting with someone who could - in my opinion - see beyond what we call reality.

As the three of us drove around, we talked. I had no idea who Baba was so I was uninhibited and asked him a million random questions. I think I was about eleven or twelve at that time. It was great fun. I was also allowed to attend some of his training sessions.

One day he was asked: "Baba, the world is such an ugly place. I want to see the world as being beautiful. What should I do?" "Look inside yourself," Baba replied. "Find God. Find light inside yourself. Find the beauty inside yourself and when you do, you will begin to see it all around you." I remember making a mental note: Got to look inside. Okay.

The next question from another student was: "Baba, I want to be a better husband, a better father. I'm a terrible person inside and I don't know what to do. What can you give me as advice?" Baba said, "Find beauty in the world. See God in everyone else. See the light. And when you do, you will see it inside yourself." He had just told the first student to look inside self. Now he was instructing students to look inside others. I looked up at him with a puzzled look on my face and he said, "You heard correctly." His point was to look both externally and internally.

THE MATRIX

The 1999 movie, The Matrix, hints at the relationship between the above (external reality) and below (internal reality). In it, the entire society (except for a few rebels) lives within a type of

internal, projected reality. The hero of the story, Neo, wakes up to realize there is another reality, an external reality behind the projections. His mission is to tap into his internal power within this external reality. How to do that is explained to him by a boy who is apparently using psychic-kinesics (his mind) to bend a spoon. The boy tells him, "Do not try and bend the spoon. That's impossible. Instead, only try to realize the truth." Neo asks, "What truth?" "There is no spoon." "There is no spoon?" "Then you'll see that it is not the spoon that bends. It is only yourself."

The quote above from the Kahuna Kapihe indicates that the below (personal reality) and the above (external reality) will be integrated by the light. Many teachers refer to The Matrix claim that its lesson is that there is no spoon. However, Neo picks up the spoon and bends it, showing a deeper lesson here. At one level (below) there is a spoon (he was holding it and bending it), yet at another level (above) there is no spoon, just your internal experience of it. Both are connected. Realizing that both perspectives are true and that you have the ability to operate or experience reality from either perspective, you can change one aspect and thus change the other.

Neo was effective because he changed his belief. However, I have had students tell me that where they live there are no jobs. Then they ask what they should do based on Huna to change that (i.e. to bend the spoon). I respond, "Maybe you should move to where there are jobs you want." Some students are shocked by this; they expect me to say something like, "Go inside and change your perspective." But that would not be 100% helpful. If you don't have a job you want, it may be because you need to live where your dream job is. Or it may be that you have a limiting belief and the job is right in front of you, but you can't see it. Or, it may be a combination of the two. With each person and each situation, the answer may be different. Huna does not say it is one answer or the other, but that it is many possibilities. The most important question is, what are you willing to do to change your experience?

DIFFERENCE VS. SIMILARITIES

So what are we to do with these seemingly separate realities, external versus internal, mine versus yours, above versus below?

Western scientific thinking would have us reduce things into their smallest separate unit. It emphasizes pulling components apart and distinguishing their unique differences as a way to understand the whole. But this line of thinking has contributed to the loss of connectedness, higher-self and spirituality.

One of the basic assumptions of Huna is: Looking for differences leads away from spirit but looking for similarities leads to spirit. When you break a concept or idea down into its various components you move away from spirit. You "earth" the energy of the idea or concept that you're experiencing. You make it solid, defined, unmoving, limited. But when you look for the similarities in ideas and concepts, you create an association, and that association draws you up and moves you toward spirit.

Like many of us growing up, my mother taught me to "Never talk about politics or religion." What she meant was, "Never bring up topics that will separate you from another."

John Ka'imikaua[2] taught the spirituality of the islands, Hawaiiana, and he chanted in honor of the ancient Hawaiian gods. And he was a

---

2 John Ka'imikaua was a hula master who carried the lineage from Moloka'i, a strong and powerful lineage from one of the most powerful islands in all of Hawaii. John taught Hula and he taught spirituality / empowerment to many people. We lost John in 2006, and we all feel the loss. John taught at our first Huna workshop in the late 80's and either he or his wife have been at every workshop to share their mana'o (their thinking or wisdom).

devout Mormon. At one point the LDS Church told him that he couldn't do Hula any more. But his response was, "The two are not conflicting, unless you choose them to be."

John taught at several of our trainings, and I once asked him how he could reconcile his Huna teaching with his Mormon beliefs. He explained by saying, "They're not in conflict with each other. They don't have to be. People create conflicts. People make the conflicts in their mind. Why should something that is so spiritual and so right and so rich a culture conflict with something that is also so positive in my life as a religion?" When you look for the similarity as John did, you actually get closer to spirit, and you no longer focus on the differences between the religions.

Never bring up topics that will separate you from another.

Usually when we have a misconception about a certain religion or path, we are focusing on the actions or beliefs of certain individuals of that faith. For example, most religions I've ever experienced believe in love and forgiveness. Though each has a different approach and different way of expressing it, Islam, Judaism, Christianity, Buddhism all teach us to be loving and to forgive ourselves and others.

But it's clear that not all people who claim a faith are actually practicing its tenets. This is a hala; these people have missed the path or erred by omission. The spiritual organization is not at fault. It is the individual's responsibility to act in accordance with the path they claim, or to get back on that path if they have fallen off. By taking on this responsibility for your own spiritual growth, you stand in your own power as John did.

VALUE OF DIFFERENCES

There are times when you have to explore differences to learn. You step into someone else's shoes to learn how they perceive the world. You read various interpretations of a political policy to understand it more fully. You take note of differences in spiritual approaches to grasp the underlying subtleties. I have studied various detailed concepts in psychology and learned from all of them. So I do believe there is a place to explore differences.

Yet to reach an agreement, to move down a spiritual path, you need to see the similarities. When I visit so many cultures during my trainings and I look around the planet, I see so much similarity. If we choose to see it, we would realize that even people on the other side of the planet think and believe the same thing. They just manifest it in a different way. Exploring differences is great as a tool for learning. But find the similarities and you find spirit.

CHOOSING WHAT YOU BELIEVE

In his book The Holographic Universe, Michael Talbot emphasized the importance of beliefs. In some ways, most of our reality boils down to what we believe. The question after this chapter is, what do you believe? Does it support you in your path? Is your belief real? Are you willing to believe something new that will support you? When you find a belief that resonates with your heart (as Huna does for me), grab it and make it yours. Once it is yours, stop caring what others think about your belief.

Another great quote from the sequel to The Matrix is rarely mentioned. However when I heard it, I felt that it summed up being pono and being on your path. Morpheus was arguing with the General what should be done to defend his home city. The General argued that everyone should stay and fight. Morpheus felt strongly that finding Neo and heading back into the Matrix was the only way to save everyone. When General said, "Not everyone believes what you believe Morpheus." Morpheus responded calmly, "My beliefs don't require them to."

That quote says a lot. It says that when you become pono, when you are calm, centered and balanced moving down your path, then you are right with your beliefs and undisturbed that other people have different beliefs. The two are not in conflict. In our Western society, we spend too much time thinking about what others think we should think. Once you find your path and you feel pono, be congruent and solid in your belief, fully knowing that the different beliefs of others have no bearing on what is true for you.

SUMMARY:

1. The vast majority of what we perceive is the product of what we expect or believe to be true.

2. Because there is too much data to absorb in any moment, our minds select, filter and generalize, picking up only a fragment of all data available.

3. Changing or challenging our beliefs can change our reality.

CHAPTER EIGHT: CAUSE & EFFECT

To gain maximum power, it is essential that we take responsibility for everything that happens in our universe, that we recognize ourselves as cause, not effect. As you begin working with this concept, it may feel overwhelming rather than empowering. But that feeling disappears when you understand the concepts meaning fully.

First of all, taking full responsibility does not mean that you are at fault or to blame for your universe. Cause and effect is not about fault or blame at all. The concept of cause and effect is very simple. From a physical standpoint, cause and effect works like this: If I bang my head against the wall, my head will hurt. And every time I bang my head against the wall, my head will hurt. That's a cause and an effect.

Here's where responsibility creates empowerment. Some people recognize that they are the cause of the head banging. They realize that they can (and should) relate to the wall differently to produce a different result. They can walk around it, over it, or build a door to go through it. But using their head as a battering ram is unlikely to be effective!

Other people remain on the effect side of the equation. "That wall is just too stubborn, strong, unconquerable. If that wall wasn't there, my head wouldn't hurt. Other people aren't stuck with walls. How come I have to bang into one? Why won't that wall disappear? I guess I'll just have to keep banging away and resign myself to a constant headache. . . " Can you relate? Which side of the cause and effect equation are you on in the various areas of your life?

Simply put, cause and effect could be viewed as "reasons versus results." On the effect side of the equation are all the reasons: the reasons why you don't have the things you desire, why you're not creating the energy you want in your life, why you're not experiencing a fuller spirituality. On the cause side of the equation, you have results. When you move yourself from the effect side to the cause side of the equation, you become empowered and you increase your results. Therefore, rather than looking at it as purely cause and effect, ask yourself, in the various areas in your life, are you getting your results (do you realize you are the cause and creator of your reality) or do you have reasons why you don't have your results?

BEYOND THE DOING

Cause and effect are easy to observe from a physical standpoint. It's clear how our physical actions cause certain effects. If you overeat and don't exercise, you often get fat. If you act as a good friend to others, you'll probably have good friends. If you drive at 60 mph in a 25 mph zone, you are likely to get a ticket.

However, most traditions, Huna included, teach that not only your actions but your thoughts and your words have creative power as well. As my father interpreted from a discussion he had with Papa Bray, "From experience, let me tell you, every word is a prayer; every thought you hold in your mind casts a spell. Every action is a magical act. Every identification is a false identification. What you hold in your mind creates a result, so everything you think, everything you say, and everything you do has consequence."

John Ka'imikaua told me that the ancients used to say, "In the word, there is life; in the word, there is death." The ancient Hawaiians were very careful with their words and thoughts, knowing the power that words and thoughts wield. John explained that they knew that the mana each person carries has the ability to put intention into action and into reality. You say or think something negative, that energy goes out then comes back to you. Uncle George Na'ope told me that the original Hawaiian language had no vulgarity and no nasty sayings. So even when you wanted to say something unkind to someone, it came out so beautifully that the words would sound lovely! Perhaps the ancient Hawaiians were trying to dispel any negativity this way. Uncle George also says that the more mana you have, the more you have to watch your intention. So in English, we might say something nice, but if our thoughts are focused on the opposite of what we said, the mana is still put out there.

> What you hold in your mind creates a result, so everything you think, everything you say, and everything you do has consequence.

Most of us are familiar with using affirmations. Affirmative statements sometimes work and sometimes do not. Why? Huna would say affirmations are only powerful and helpful if the affirmation is pono and equally experienced on all levels. For example, if you say "I am happy" but you have overwhelming sadness that you have avoided releasing or facing, your affirmation is only on the surface. If affirmations alone worked, I would be teaching them and only them! Affirmations are very powerful examples of principles of the Law of Attraction that work only after you are pono and aligned inside and out with that which you are affirming.

Regarding the power of words and thoughts, my father, Tad Kiaina'auaomalkalani James, once wrote, "Take care in what you ask for. Take care, for there are consequences for what you receive. Situations which are not win-win often require a payback. Every successful pule (prayer) may have the potential to reduce your freedom and increase your bondage because of your attachment to the result of the pule. That is why you should incorporate your awaiku (good spirits that are a part of our Huna lineage) in your pule."

The Now

Huna says that you are the cause of your present, your now, and that your now is your place of power. As you stand in your now, the future is before you and the past is behind you. Whoever you are right now in this moment is the sum total of all the decisions you've made in the past as well as thoughts you have about the future. Those two things have collided into what we perceive as now. Consciously or unconsciously, you have chosen to experience exactly what you're experiencing right now in this moment, either by something you've done in the past or something you're thinking about doing in the future.

Of course, because you are only able to experience the now, that reality is actually created in this moment. However, since we experience our lives in a linear sequence, most of us have an easier time realizing that we are a sum total of our past and future. This means that at some level you created everything around you. Knowing that you have caused this result, you realize that you can change it. And you have additional power in that you can choose how you wish to react to what you've created.

Choosing Your Reactions

September 11, 2001 is often cited as an extreme example of cause and effect. Am I saying that 9/11 is your fault or that you caused it? No. The ancients didn't believe that they had enough power to cause an event like that. But they knew that they were in total control of what they experienced. And they knew that when you experience any event or circumstance in life, you are definitely in charge of your reactions to it.

The late John Ka'imikaua was a Hawaiian culture master who carried the lineage of Moloka'i. The only time that John and his wife Ka'oi could not attend our Huna training was during the week of September 11th. John understood this idea of cause and effect even though he had never studied Huna. His response to the attack was, "What a tragic event, and my heart goes out to the victims. How terrible that we as a race living on the same planet have created this event. What do we need to learn from this event to come together as a people so that we can create the world we want? How do we now move forward?" He said, "If we don't get the learning, we're just going to repeat it again."

That's cause and effect. Cause and effect is saying, "I am responsible for what I am getting in my life." If not for creating the event or circumstance itself, then at least we are responsible for our reaction to it. We're responsible for what we're getting in our lives. We are the cause. We project our world out around us. We are responsible for creating all the negative and all the positive that's happening in our lives. We can be at cause and still, of course, have amazing compassion for others as John did.

RESPONSIBILITY FOR CHANGE

In ancient times, the Kahuna would not do any healing work if there was anyone present in the room who did not believe or who was there simply to prove that the concepts didn't work. The Kahuna was less concerned with skepticism than he was committed to the concept that the energy of healing isn't outside the group but generated from within. Additionally, keeping a space sacred for this type of work insured that only the beliefs of the Kahuna and the individual seeking the assistance from the Kahuna were present.

Huna healing also requires full participation from the one being healed. Huna teaches that only you can make the change you seek. It cannot be given to you. A Kahuna can guide, instruct, open the path for you. But he will not walk the path for you. John Ka'imikaua talked about his aunt, a healer who said that there needed to be three things present for a healing to take place. First, there had to be permission. Without permission, there was no space and/or connection to do the work. Second, there needed to be an acknowledgement from the person receiving the healing that the energy and/or healing came from a higher source. This source could be aumakua, higher self, God, or anything that was within the belief system of the individual. And finally, the person had to acknowledge the Kahuna was just a conduit, channel, or caller of the energy rather than the source of it. So while people would seek out Kahuna because they were experts in healing, the healing itself was a "do with," not a "do to" process.

Like many systems, Huna says that power comes from within. It is already present in each of us and waiting to be tapped. There are no exceptions. As you begin to own that power and realize that you can create your world exactly as you want it, your unconscious mind will accept your evaluation as truth and act accordingly.

Some of us are called to tap into it, others want guidance from a Kahuna or expert to tap into it.

The Lost Secrets of Ancient Hawaiian Huna[1] says that there is a rain barrel of pure energy hovering over the top of our heads. As human beings, we must try to draw all of that energy through the eye dropper of our neurology. It's our responsibility to bring that energy in, feel it and work with it. There is so much energy, yet we rarely take the time to open ourselves up to expanding our neurology beyond that eye dropper.

There is an abundance of energy available to us. But when we first begin to acknowledge it and draw it in, we may feel uncertain. Rather than thinking "I'm not feeling the energy," think "I'm working at feeling it more." Be mindful of what you say to yourself as you begin the process, and know that your neurology might take time to open up. Rather than focusing on whether or not you're feeling it, begin to notice whatever subtle differences you experience. Notice what instructions you give yourself, what you say to yourself. Notice how you accept or reject information. Notice how you perceive the world around you. With just some subtle changes you could begin to see and experience the universe exactly the way you want to. You have become cause. You are fully responsible.

James, T. (1997). The Lost Secrets of Ancient Hawaiian Huna. Honolulu, HI: Advanced Neuro Dynamics.

BEING AT CAUSE

Look at the areas in your life., Do you have reasons or results? Are you willing to give them up? Because happy successful people give up their reasons and go for what they desire, and they get their results. I took my 9 year-old son to see the movie The Pursuit of Happyness as an example of this. To see that others can do something magnificent in life and step out above and beyond what is expected is inspiring for us all.

Quite often we wait for something to happen to us rather than taking charge. I have been very fortunate in my journeys to learn from masters and wonderful teachers. One important lesson they taught me was to take initiative and act, especially on guidance from my higher self.

Once while traveling to Pembroke Ontario Canada to conduct a weekend training, my gut (higher self) told me I should bring a gift with me. So I brought a kukui nut lei, a lei that represents the light made by Auntie Bernie, even though I had no idea why I brought it.

When I arrived, a spiritual leader from the Native Canadian tribe came to greet me with a smudging ceremony and a peace pipe ceremony. He had had a dream about someone visiting. When he saw me, he said I looked more white in person. In the middle of the ceremony he asked me to chant the chant I do. Without missing a beat, I chanted the chant to higher self, to creator. When I had finished, he asked if the chant was to the creator as it had been in his dream. During the ceremony, he presented me with an eagle feather which was a great honor. Of course, I had the special lei to offer as a gift in return, only because I had taken action based on my gut feeling.

An interesting point about the eagle feather: The eagle feather represents achieving a certain level or perspective in life, and yet the eagle has the ability to come back down to earth with that perspective. Receiving this feather reaffirmed that I was on my right path. It was explained to me that the feather is given only after a certain level of consciousness has already been achieved. Sometimes we are deluded into thinking "If I just had that feather (or that title or that degree), I could be who I want to be and do what I need to do." Yet, the feather never comes from desiring the feather itself. Once we give up our belief we need something external to make us whole and empowered, then and only then do we become empowered and at cause for our reality. The feather or object we previously so desired, then simply appears. At that point, we feel, "Oh,

that is nice, but I don't need this to know who I am. I know that already."

SUMMARY:

1. You are the center of your universe.

2. We all have the option to experience ourselves as cause or as effect in our lives.

3. The power to change and evolve is within each of us – no exceptions.

CHAPTER NINE: THE MIND BODY CONNECTION

In ancient times, Hawaiians didn't have to talk about the mind-body connection. It was simply a way of life. The ancient Hawaiians had a unique way of understanding the mind-body connection. They agreed with Western thinking that the unconscious mind is responsible for preserving and running the physical body. But they did not believe that physical ailments or issues are caused by physiological malfunctions alone.

Huna would say the physical goes awry because of the mixed messages we give the unconscious. For instance, we say we want to be healthy, but then we eat unhealthy foods. We say we want to feel energized but we don't take time to rest. When the unconscious mind gets conflicting messages, it may stop working properly, follow the message that is the easiest, or even begin to create malfunctions because of the confusion. From the Huna perspective, this is the basis of all physiological disease, not

germs or viruses or aging, so disease cannot be explained or fixed on the physical alone.

While getting my doctorate in psychology, I learned some contemporary disciplines that explore this phenomenon as well. Psychoneuroimmunology (PNI) looks at the mind/body connection and, rather than saying illness is all physical, the relationship between the physical and the mind is investigated. For example, if I get an infection, I'll go to an MD, an expert on the physical level. I'll take some antibiotics and maybe extra vitamin C and other supplements because I know my body needs vitamins, minerals and supplements to promote health.

But if within a short span of time, I get multiple infections and the MD doesn't know why, or if the medicine does not work, then both Huna and PNI would say that the problem may be beyond the physical. In ancient times, a medical/physical practitioner and psychological/ spiritual practitioner would work together for healing. It was known that our minds, emotions, and spirits were not separate from our bodies. Today, many in the healing professions are moving back toward this holistic or integrative approach, working in collaboration with others who have different areas of expertise. My expertise is in the realm of Huna, the spiritual, mental and emotional, and how it trickles down into the physical. I work with other experts when the problem is beyond my scope. This is often known as integrative medicine or integrative psychology.

Every cell in your body is eavesdropping on your internal dialogue.

As neuroscience has shown, input to your senses, including a directive or desire from your conscious mind, creates an electrical impulse. As soon as the impulse gets to the end of a neural pathway, it releases a chemical. Researchers say that this chemical is then picked up by every cell in your body. As Deepak Chopra puts it, "Every cell in your body is eavesdropping on your internal dialogue."

So not only do you not want to have conflicting messages, you want the right messages so they release the right chemical. If you want to raise the energy vibration in your body, you've got to do something to get the right electrical impulses to trickle down into the physical.

One of the ways the ancients did this was by chanting. They knew that the vibration of certain words had a positive impact on the body. They also knew that every thought you have, everything that you do or say — in other words how you perceive your world — trickles down into the physical. From the Huna perspective, we should ask ourselves, "What am I creating in my head and what chemicals are those thoughts releasing, trickling down into the physical?"

TRICKLE DOWN

I use the phrase "trickle down" not only because of the chemical release through your system, but also because in Huna, like most esoteric systems, it is believed that the plane above the plane with which you're working is the controlling or directing plane. So if you're working with the physical, the plane above the physical actually has a certain level of control over it and in part directs it. Huna says that you have conscious control over your physical body but the emotional body rules the physical body. The emotional body then is ruled by the mental body, and the mental body is ruled by the spiritual body. This means that if the higher self or spiritual body has a desire or message, it will trickle all the way down to the physical.

Have you ever known someone who gave up everything for a spiritual journey or a spiritual path? When the spiritual body kicks in and it's your dharma to do it, everything falls into alignment and it just happens. Other people may not be able to make sense of such a move and say that the individual is crazy for giving up everything to go on their quest. But the spiritual body controls all the planes beneath it.

This is one of the reasons the Kahuna only worked on someone with permission. They know that a person's mental body controls the emotional body. Unless the mental body is in agreement, the mental body can block the emotional body from releasing an emotional issue. To explain from a psychological perspective, a limiting decision or belief can prevent you from releasing a negative emotion. For example, if someone believes strongly that only a priest can absolve them of their guilt, that belief of the mental body will block the emotional body from releasing guilt without a priest's blessing. If someone believes that releasing anger toward another is a sign of weakness, he or she will not be able to release anger. The mental body controls the emotional.

Similarly, the emotional body rules the physical. We've all seen people who have maintained negative emotions over a prolonged period and witnessed the effects to their physical bodies. Emotional stress creates damaging physiological consequences all the way down to the quantum. The Hawaiians believe that any physical issue also affects the other bodies because they're all interrelated. Therefore, the best healing begins from the highest plane possible. Ho'oku'u (literally "to make release / let go") or higher self therapy is most effective because it incorporates the spiritual body and trickles down through all of the others.

HO'OKU'U (HIGHER SELF THERAPY)

The highest plane, the one that governs all the planes beneath it, is your higher self (Chapter Four) which is related to your spiritual body. Like most governing bodies, the higher self has a set of directives by which it operates. Up until now, you've managed to survive without understanding these directives or even knowing that they exist. Yet, as mentioned earlier, ignorance of the law is not an adequate defense. You can't complain about your life if you are unwilling to learn the governing rules. Knowing them will help you connect with the higher self and, through it, the energy available to you in the universe to rebalance the four bodies for your healing.

PRIME DIRECTIVES OF HIGHER SELF

1. Aumakua acts as a totally trustworthy parental spirit over the individual.

2. It is the representation of the God spirit within the individual. (The outer expression of the God spirit is called Kane.)

3. Connection or communication with higher self can make everything pono, right, clear, good and aligned.

4. Aumakua is perfectly balanced male-female energy.

5. It is an expression of every man and woman's perfection. Ancient text says that when the conscious mind grows up and evolves to become a higher conscious mind, it is the perfection of who and what we really are and what we can be.

6. Aumakua is the connection that allows all creation. Anything we create on the physical level begins somehow, someway in the spiritual. We may not be aware of this spark of creation until it trickles down to the conscious mind as an idea or desire. But its beginning was prior to our conscious awareness.

7. The higher self represents the process of evolution in Huna.

8. Aumakua has the power to recognize root causes. When releasing negative emotion, we call on aumakua through unihipili: "Dear unconscious mind, please light up all the anger (fear, hatred, etc) including the root cause, the first event so that aumakua can recognize the cause and facilitate a release."

9. It has the power to remove fixations and identifications.

10. It has the power to produce empowerment of the senses, which in the Eastern systems were called siddhis.

11. Aumakua can know, predict and affect the future.

12. The higher self does not make mistakes.

13. Aumakua will not interfere with conscious mind's free will. (Unconscious mind will also not interfere with conscious mind's free will.)

CREATING THE CONNECTION

With all that the higher self has to offer and knowing that its effects trickle down throughout your entire system, doesn't it seem worth it to make connection with the aumakua a priority? So how do we do it? Well, to begin, acknowledge that you have a higher self and that you are already connected with it. Of course, there are chants, ceremonies and mediations that strengthen this connection, but they would be difficult to guide you through in a book. However, there are some simple things you can do to begin to connect with and experience your higher self.

One simple starting point is to find what resonates with your spirit. Uncle George always expressed the importance of finding and doing what feels good and right to you. Take a moment now to remember a time where you experienced a spiritual moment. I have taught the concepts of Huna to thousands of students. Whenever I ask my groups "How many of you have had a spiritual experience?" well over 90% of the hands in the room go up. So I know most of us have had at least one we would describe as spiritual.

As you think of that moment, what was going on? What were you seeing, hearing and feeling? Can you recapture the feeling of that moment so you are able to experience it again? By reliving it and feeling the presence of higher self, you can begin to recognize when your higher self is wanting to talk with you.

Another avenue of connection to higher self is through dance, hula, and chanting. There are also other activities that you may do that help to connect with your spirit and allow the manaloa to flow such as communing with nature or listening to beautiful music.

Yet another way of creating that mind-body connection is meditation. Meditation changes the energy traveling across neural pathways. It too trickles all the way down into the physical. Personally, I have spent a lot of my life studying and practicing meditation. Spending time with a meditation that works for you enhances the mind-body connection as well as the connection with the higher self.

Find my guided meditation CD at http://www.Huna.com or email info@huna.com to assist with the process.

The key is to just begin, to do anything that helps open the connection with higher self.

SUMMARY:

1. All physical disease is caused by imbalance in the four bodies or miscommunication between the three minds.

2. The best therapy comes from the highest plane possible, aumakua (indwelling God-self).

3. There are various forms to help connect with aumakua. Finding a form that feels right for you is key.

CHAPTER TEN: PONO AND THE AKA CONNECTION

I've touched on the concept of pono in previous chapters. To the ancient Hawaiians, being pono was not just a good idea. It was essential to their way of being. In part, this is because they believed that they were connected to all things and each other – a belief which quantum physics has now "proven" to be true. So to be out of synch or at odds with anyone or any thing was to be at odds with your self.

Pono is one of those Hawaiian words that doesn't have a good English translation. A popular translation for the word pono would be "right" but not as in "I'm right, you're wrong." Pono is a state of being, of being right with yourself. It is a feeling of having unwavering congruency about yourself, about others, or about a situation.

I think we've all had that experience when we felt as though we were standing in our own power. You knew at the deepest level that you are right with who and what you are. In that moment, any effort to persuade you otherwise was pointless. That's pono. When you are pono with

yourself, you feel a level of congruency with your path, with what you are doing. When you are pono with someone else, everything is clear and comfortable between the two of you. When you are pono with your environment, you feel a sense of well-being, ease. When you are pono, you feel connected on all levels.

AKA

The concept of pono and the process of ho'oponopono (often called the Hawaiian forgiveness process) were taught to my father by Papa Bray and by Morrnah Simeona.[1] Both Papa Bray and Morrnah Simeona believed that

---

1 *Morrnah Simeona taught the process of ho'oponopono to hundreds if not thousands of people in Hawai'i and around the world. She was designated a Living Golden Treasure by the Governor and Hawai'i State legislature for her work in this area and was invited to speak with the members of the United Nations and the World Health Organization on the subject of forgiveness and ho'oponopono. (The foundation that continues her work is called The Foundation of I, and may be found at www.hooponopono.org.)*

you are intimately connected to everyone with whom you come into contact and to everything around you. This is the aka connection.

The literal translation for aka is "sticky stuff," like stepping on freshly chewed gum on a hot sidewalk. Aka is an etheric substance that can stretch indefinitely. It is a conduit for holding the mana (energy), like the insulation surrounding an electrical wire on the metaphysical level. Papa Bray said without aka, energy would just disperse back into the universe. Like the insulation around a wire, aka contains and directs the energy current.

The instant you touch something, a connection is formed and the energy flow between you and the other begins as soon as that aka connection is formed. It works like an alternating current (AC). In other words, the energy doesn't flow in just one direction; it flows in two directions, from you and to you. Just like AC. There are many subtleties to this current, what it is and how it works. But for now, it's just important to know that this exchange of energy is immediate.

Beginning students often tell me that they don't feel this connection, probably because they have a certain expectation of how that energy connection is supposed to feel. But I'd bet that we've all experienced it. Have you ever been in a crowd and suddenly felt that someone was staring at you? You turn and immediately pick that person out of the crowd, even though there may be a hundred other people present. How did you spot that person so quickly? Because at the unconscious level you can trace the aka connection created by his or her focus toward you back to them. It is your unconscious mind that is in charge and aware of all of your aka connections, not your conscious mind.

Have you ever known that the phone was going to ring before it rang? Or had a sense of who was calling before you answered it? That's because mana flowing through aka works more swiftly than AT&T (no offense intended to AT&T – I certainly wouldn't want them to cut off my phone service!). On the unconscious level, you feel that energy coming in. Or perhaps you have thought about someone and almost immediately, she calls you. In that case, your thoughts about the other person sends energy to her. Unconsciously, she feels it and has an urge to call you. That's how mana flowing through aka works.

The aka connection may be more obvious with people you know well. You can finish one another's sentences; you immediately fall into synch when walking together; you sense his mood with little interaction. But whether we are aware of it or not, we have the aka connection with everyone. Anyone we touch, anyone we notice, anyone with whom we communicate whether verbally or non-verbally, these all create a connection and an energy exchange. At the metaphysical level, you are exchanging mana with these people.

In the Huna workshops, I teach that "energy flows where attention goes." I have heard this in many systems and find it absolutely true when working with energy. Even the tiniest bit of attention – a glance, brushing by someone on a busy street, reading about someone in the newspaper – creates an aka connection. Every connection you've ever made is still with you today unless you have consciously done something to cut that connection. That means every person you've made eye contact with at the grocery store or who has sat next to you on a plane is still connected to you. It's incredible to think about, a little overwhelming in fact!

During my time in Japan I was challenged by how small my personal space had become. In Aikido, there is a concept of ma-ai, which is the distance between you and another person where it feels comfortable to interact. The cultural ma-ai in Japan was much closer than I was used to in Hawai'i. I stood in a line one day and the person behind me stood so close that we were almost touching. When I stepped forward to give myself more space, he immediately stepped forward with me. His energy was palpable! If I hadn't cut that connection (I'll explain how we cut the connection in the next chapter), I would still be connected to that person and there would still be an energy exchange taking place.

ARE THERE BAD CONNECTIONS?

I've heard people say, "You need to do certain things to keep negative energies out and do certain things to keep positive energies in." But Papa Bray said that his father, Daddy Bray, was very clear about this. He didn't believe that energy or your connection to other people was either negative or positive. It can be negative or positive from a polarity perspective, as with a battery. But to say that energy is good or bad would be like looking at a 9-volt battery and declaring, "Here's the good side (the plus). And here's the bad side (the minus)." If the battery could think, it would consider you crazy!

Yet many systems talk about negative energy or positive energy. I think what's been lost in the translation is that the intent or thought can be positive or negative. When people have negative intentions, that intention goes into the energy. It's also true that as soon as you label something negative, you actually put negativity into the energy. But in and of itself, energy is just energy. Like electricity, which you can use to light a bulb or to electrocute someone. That does not make the electricity good or bad; the intent or use of it defines that.

There may be times when you want to disconnect from individuals because the connection may not be the best thing for you. For example, I have had a close friend since high school who has become a very successful woman. She is a mother of three, handles the house and has just completed a nursing degree. When she is just with me or with her peers, she stands in her own light. She is articulate, intelligent, confident. Yet when her father walks in the room, she transforms into a little girl again. I see her confidence disappear and she seems unable to express herself. I tried to talk to her about it once saying, "You know what happens when you get around your dad . . ." Before I could finish my sentence, she said, "I know, I'm daddy's little girl."

So for my friend, the time is ripe to cut the connection. Not because the connection itself is bad, but because that connection holds her to the past. By cutting the old connection and establishing a new one with her father, she will be able to enjoy a new adult relationship with him and allow him to experience the beautiful woman she has become. But the aka connection itself is not good or bad.

Cutting connections from a metaphysical standpoint is not only practical but recommended. My recommendation is to cut your connection to everyone in your life on a regular basis. Why? Because, as I learned from my lineage and Morrnah Simeona, the old aka connection colors and filters your perception of the other person. You see the young child who was a sickly infant as vulnerable and fragile. You don't trust a co-worker's judgment because of a mistake made long ago. You remember the parent who protected and nurtured you so you become impatient when they become elderly and frail. Even if someone is shining as the brightest light on the planet, you may have trouble seeing it because your perception is being pushed through an old

aka connection. Cutting the aka connection will change your projections onto the person, allowing you to see them more clearly for who and what they are now, instead of who they were in the past.

When I do group training programs, each night I do ho'oponopono (the process described in the next chapter) to disconnect from the participants. I want them to stand in their own power. If I give energy in any way, shape, or form, I won't see the transformation that's taken place each morning when the students return to class. If that old connection is there, I may not see that change.

My wife and I cut the aka connection between us on a regular basis. The instant that we disconnect, we think of each other, look at each other or touch each other to reestablish a connection. Morrnah Simeona believed that you should cut the aka connection with everyone, regardless of who they are, regardless of how long you have been connected. She said, "If you've been in a marriage for 20 years and you haven't cut the aka connection, you should." Why? You create a new connection and therefore see the person for who they are, not who they've been. When you make a brand-new connection it will be just as strong, if not stronger, as the old one. On the metaphysical level, twenty years doesn't make a connection any stronger than a brand-new one with a fresh charge of energy. Actually, twenty years can make the connection less strong. Imagine re-connecting with a person you love very much from choice in a moment of empowerment. That new connection will be stronger than the old one!

You also want to make sure you do ho'oponopono to cut the aka connection with your children on a regular basis. Of course, there are times when you wouldn't want to cut the aka connection. A newborn child needs to retain a constant exchange of energy. But when children get to a certain age, you might want to do it every five minutes! When my daughter was only a week old, she kept me up for 5 days straight. I practiced ho'oponopono a lot in those hours! When your children have grown and left home, the process will allow you to reconnect with them as adults. You may still experience some empty nest pangs but the transition will be easier.

When you do this with a loved one who is not present with you, call them or think of them after you've cut the aka connection so you can reconnect. If they happen to be sensitive to energy, they might call you first. My mom has never done any of these trainings, but she's so intuitive that as soon as I cut my aka connection with her, she phones me and says, "Hi, sweetie. Just wanted to reconnect. Felt like we hadn't been in touch for awhile."

Beyond loved ones and those with whom we interact regularly, it's important to cut the aka connection with people in general. Since energy isn't positive or negative, you may wonder why you need to disconnect from people you don't know, passing strangers or slight acquaintances. There can be what we might label as negative consequences by remaining connected to any person or large group. In the Hawaiian system, you cut the aka connection. Then you would have the option to reestablish it with individuals you choose. This practice puts you in charge of your connections.

Morrnah Simeona also believed that when a person passes away, you should cut the aka connection immediately and make a new connection with the memories. On her deathbed, she instructed all of her students to do this. "As soon as I pass, disconnect because I will no longer be on this plane with you. My energy vibration will be different, which means I may draw your energy, or you may draw mine and not let me evolve to another level." She said, "Cut the aka connection, and remember the positive memories."

I have been practicing this for years and when my grandmother passed away in 2002, I experienced a deep sadness and grief. I did the ho'oponopono process (when it felt appropriate to do so) to cut the aka connection then I reconnected with my fond memories of her. Cutting the aka connection doesn't make you emotionless but allows your emotions at a time like that to be expressed in a more positive, appropriate way.

So now that you understand the importance of cutting the aka connection, how do we do it? It's not enough to just say, "Okay, I'm disconnecting from you." Cutting the aka connection is done within the process of ho'oponopono, described in the next chapter. But there is more to the Huna concept of connectedness than the energy exchange between people.

CONNECTION TO ALL THINGS

Connectedness does not only apply to people but to all living things. In ancient Hawai'i, people didn't just go chop a tree down. In the Hawaiian system (as quantum physics has discovered) everything is alive and everything is a projection of you. If you treat something outside of yourself with disrespect, you're treating yourself with disrespect – and you're asking for that disrespectful energy to come back to you. So the Hawaiians first talked to a tree they wished to cut and connected via pule, a form of prayer mentioned previously.

My Kumu Hula (teacher of Hula) Etua, told me a story about a Hawaiian canoe builder. The name Hokule'a was given to a canoe that was built in Hawai'i to verify that you could navigate from Hawai'i to Tahiti without modern equipment. They needed a hull that was strong enough and well-balanced enough to sail to Tahiti without any modern instruments. According to the story, a canoe practitioner (in ancient times, he may have been called a Kahuna) went

into the forest and found the tree that would be perfect for the main hull of such a canoe. As he looked at it, he paid attention to the birds and one showed him which tree to use. Although he knew it was meant to be, the tree was alive and the builder, Nainoa Thompson, knew better than to just grab a chain saw (or whatever they had at that time) and cut it down.

So the canoe builder and the practitioner went together into the forest and made an offering to the tree. They put the offering at the tree's base, and the practitioner addressed the tree. "If you would like, we would love to work with you and have you become the hull of this canoe. Here's the purpose, here's the reason." They did a pule and left. Some time later, they went back into the forest to discover that the tree had laid itself down. It hadn't hit any other trees in the area but had snapped off at exactly the point where the canoe builder wanted to cut it. They took the tree out without disturbing anything else and built the Hokule'a. They had connected with the tree through pule, the process of working with, calling out to or praying to living things, the energies and the elements.

BEFORE CONTINUING

Before continuing to the next chapter, it is important to grasp that it is really healthy and helpful to cut your aka connections. These connections can be remade again and again. In fact, by reforming these connections while you are pono, you will be making stronger more congruent connections. The next chapter talks about how to cut them, so make sure you are ready for the process as you continue.

SUMMARY:

1. To become pono – aligned, congruent, right – is not just a good idea but essential.

2. We are connected to all beings. To do harm to others is to harm ourselves.

3. Though we form aka connections with everyone and everything in our sphere, we can be in charge of these connections.

Chapter Eleven: Ho'oponopono

Ho'oponopono is the process that allows you to cut the aka connection and create a new one. Huna teaches that the ho'oponopono process is essential if you wish to be pono through life.

As previously mentioned, Ho'oponopono is often called the Hawaiian forgiveness process. The Hawaiian word ho'oponopono comes from ho'o ("to make") and pono ("right"). The repetition of the word pono means "doubly right" or being right with both self and others (i.e. as above, so below). In a nutshell, ho'oponopono is a process by which you forgive others to whom you are connected. You energetically cut the aka connection in a very positive, loving way, from the heart with aloha, knowing that you can make the connection brand new. When you become right with others, you become right with yourself. It's important not only from an interpersonal perspective but from a metaphysical standpoint as well.

When I went back to school to pursue my PhD, I picked ho'oponopono as my research focus because this is more than just a concept that I teach. It is a part of my family lineage and how I live my life. People had said to me, "This ho'oponopono sounds great, but where is the proof?"

I gave a lecture to a Hawaiian studies group at the University of Hawaii about my Huna lineage and about ho'oponopono. I started the talk by describing my lineage and my particular kumu (teachers). At the very end, I mentioned I had researched ho'oponopono for my doctoral degree. I intentionally shared in this particular order because, though Western thinking may want proof and statistics, in the ancient culture, lineage and practice was more important. The fact that my doctoral research validated the process was simply "icing on the cake" as one of the professors noted.

Within the state of Hawai'i, we have four counties, each having city and county governments. The reason for breaking Hawai'i into four counties dates back hundreds of years when there were four kingdoms, the kingdoms of Hawai'i, Maui, O'ahu. and Kauai. There are smaller island kingdoms as well, but the four big ones were the most prominent.

If the kings of these kingdoms didn't happen to like each other, there would be no communication between the islands for hundreds of years. So even though the islands were close together geographically, each island's culture grew in a slightly different direction. In fact, when the missionaries arrived early in the nineteenth century, the Hawaiian language sounded to them as though there were four different dialects.

I share this brief history because it explains why the process of ho'oponopono is done so differently on the different islands. As described by Victoria Shook[1] (1992), ho'oponopono was conducted face to face in many families. On some islands, if you have someone with whom you aren't pono, you ask another person to facilitate a meeting between the two of you, usually someone in the family. The facilitator allows each person time to express themselves,

_____
1 Shook is one of the few authors who has written about ho'oponopono for use in working with others. Though there are many authors, Shook is one of the earliest writers to have done research and presented case studies.

to get whatever the issue is off their chests, let it go, and then move forward together. To become pono.

On the other end of the spectrum, ho'oponopono can be a process you experience within your mind only. You disconnect then reconnect, if you choose to do so, internally. There are a variety of methods of ho'oponopono between these two variations, but the approach from my lineage that I share in my trainings and in this book occurs within the mind. Without going into too much statistical data here, the research I conducted on ho'oponopono has validated the process itself and the ability for individuals to benefit by doing the process within their own in their minds.

My study included a test group (a group who experienced ho'oponopono) and a control group (the group who did not experience the process). The research measured unforgiveness (which is defined in psychology as motivations for revenge and avoidance). The measurement was taken before the application of the process, immediately after, and two weeks later. The test and control group were compared.

Simply put, the research shows that there was a statistically significant reduction in unforgiveness for the group who experienced ho'oponopono. My dissertation research has been published. (If interested in it, you may contact our office 1-800-800-MIND.)

FORGIVENESS

The Hawaiian concept of forgiveness is different than forgiveness in Western culture. First of all, in Huna forgiveness is not complete until there is a complete letting go or release of the issue. And Etua always says, "You forgive. You forget the incident. You remember only the learning. You remember what it is that you need to do in order to create your universe the way that you want."

But in Western culture, after a husband and wife have a heated discussion, they both might say that they're sorry and make peace. Yet when another argument begins a week later, the husband says "See, you're just as hostile as you were last week." The wife retorts, "What does this have to do with last week? You're just holding a grudge because I was right." Neither of them had totally let go of the prior fight. As Auntie Bertie used to say, "If you don't forget, you haven't really forgiven." True pono doesn't happen when the forgiveness occurs. It happens when you forgive and you let it go.

It is important to emphasize here that letting it go, releasing it, or forgetting it, does not negate wise discernment. Even in ancient times, if a person wronged you, you forgave him or her. But then from a place of being pono, you could make the decision about how you would relate to that person going forward. A common misconception about forgiveness is that you have to become the forgiven person's best buddy!

Forgiveness means that you are flat, carrying no emotional charge about a transgression or act whereby someone wronged you. From that clear perspective, you are able to make a decision about what is right for you and any future relationship.

Forgiveness in Hawai'i must also be mutual. In the West, it's assumed that one party apologizes, the other accepts the apology. Most commonly though, one person says, "I'm sorry" while the other person thinks, "You certainly are, you sorry son of a . . .!" It's less common that there is a sincere response of "Apology accepted." But Hawaiians believe that it is best to get closure on an argument by saying "E Kala mai ia'u", which means "Please forgive me if I have done anything wrong." Saying it this way volleys responsibility to the other person and calls for action from them. It opens up an energetic connection. Instead of a one sided admission of guilt and repentance, it encourages a two way communication. In a sense, E Kala mai ia'u says, "It's in your lap."

Hawaiians also believe that everything should be forgiven, no exception. Even the most egregious transgression is to be forgiven. The justice system in ancient Hawai'i could be swift and firm. Some crimes were punishable by death and others required banishment from society. But even these transgressions were to be forgiven because, according to John Ka'imikaua, the Hawaiians believed that holding on to un-forgiveness only harms yourself.

The Hawaiian code of forgiveness says that there were three types of transgressions, all of which required forgiveness. The first is hala which means that you have "missed the path" or "erred by omission." A hala could be that you procrastinated getting something done or you weren't as clear as you could be in communicating. Perhaps you were unaware of someone else's feelings or didn't give a project your best efforts. Maybe you forgot your wedding anniversary! You commit a hala to yourself whenever you feel guilty, repress emotions, or allow someone to ignore your personal boundaries. You can commit hala without even knowing it.

The second transgression, hewa, is another offense you can commit unknowingly. Hewa means to "go overboard" or "to excess." You commit hewa when you are being a perfectionist or are obsessed with anything. Hewa could be an addiction or an obstinately held opinion. It might be overeating, drinking too much, or monopoliz-ing a conversation. Even being overly passionate about an issue and accidentally upsetting some-one with a different view is considered hewa. Hewa to yourself might be holding feelings of anger or hatred, or wanting revenge.

Clearly, hala and hewa are easy transgressions to commit, knowingly and unknowingly. When I speak to a group, I've been taught to ask for forgiveness for anything that I may have said or may say that offends anyone listening. My inten-tion is simply to share my mana'o (my thinking) with aloha. But everyone has a different reality so I don't know if I do a hala or hewa while teach-ing. No matter how pure your intention, you may be misunderstood. But if you are coming from aloha, from the heart, ho'oponopono is easy to do.

The third transgression requiring forgiveness is 'ino. 'Ino means "to do intentional harm to someone with hate in mind." It includes every-thing from vicious gossip to murder. Internally, an 'ino might be harsh self-judgment or self-dep-recation. In the Hawaiian code of forgiveness, you still have to forgive for an 'ino, no matter how big or heinous the crime. If you do not forgive, you can not be truly pono. Again, you only hurt one person by holding on to your unforgiveness and that is yourself.

THE HO'OPONOPONO PROCESS

As I mentioned, the ho'oponopono process of my lineage is a mental process. Healing yourself is the first step. To do this, imagine an infinite source of love, healing energy or white light over the top of your head. Let that energy or light pour into your head and down through your body to completely heal yourself. Let it fill up your body from your toes to your head, then let it pour out over the outside of your body so you are healed and loved inside and out.

While continuing to draw the healing light flow into yourself, construct a stage in your mind's eye. Imagine yourself floating in the air and construct the stage below and in front of you. You can construct the stage in whatever form you want.

After you've completely healed yourself and the light is overflowing from the top of your head, invite onto the stage the person with whom you want to become pono. Bring him or her on to your stage and begin step number two, the forgiveness exchange. To begin the forgiveness exchange, allow the healing, loving light to flow through your heart to this person on the stage. Allow this energy to fill them up completely. Then, even if there is no apparent need for forgiveness, you say, "Please forgive me. I forgive you too." Or you may choose to reverse the words and say, "I forgive you. Please forgive me too." Use the phrase that feels most comfortable to you.

It's possible that you might feel some resistance from the other person. Once during ho'oponopono I said, "Please forgive me," and I could feel that the person did not accept my apology. So I began a conversation, asking that person why she didn't accept my apology, what she wanted to say to me or explain, and how she felt. It's no different than clarifying any interpersonal communication. If you feel resistance, open up the dialogue before proceeding. Morrnah would remind us that this process is in your head.

Because this process is happening in your own head, in many ways the healing is between you and an aspect of yourself, not the other person. Also, check to see if the resistant person needs more of the healing light. Maybe they are not fully healed up yet.

When you've have felt the forgiveness, both to you and from you with the person on the stage, thank the person for being in your life and helping you down your path. We so often forget to thank others in our lives for being present, even if the only purpose of their presence was to help you with a learning.

When you feel that you have completed the forgiveness process, and you have said everything you needed to say with the person on the stage and have offered and received forgiveness, you are ready to cut the aka connection. Visualize the aka cord going out from your body toward the person on the stage. Next, imagine a blade of white light coming out of the source of infinite love healing energy. Let the blade float down in front of you and allow it to gently, lovingly and completely cut the connection between you and the individual on the stage. As the aka connection is cut, allow the blade to disappear beneath your feet. After that, let the person on the stage disappear, let the stage disappear, and let all remaining aka disappear.

Remember that this is taking place in your mind. This isn't an actual person on your stage. From a Jungian perspective, it is the projection of the person or the archetype of the person you hold inside yourself. You can never truly know a person for who and what they really are, even the people you know intimately. Every second you'll only see 126 bits of them. Whatever you think they are, they're more than that.

So during ho'oponopono, what you see on stage is an aspect of you. We carry inside us archetypes. If you carry a powerful archetype and recognize it, you can bring it on stage, forgive and cut the connection to shift your energetic relationship with that archetype. Who do you really forgive in this process? Yourself. And by forgiving an archetype you've projected onto another person then cutting the aka connection, it also transforms how you see the person and can make a profound difference in your relationship.

When you disconnect, in many circumstances you may choose to make a new connection. To make this new aka connection, you simply have to think of the person. The connection you've had with one another is on the metaphysical level. It existed before the ho'oponopono process, which means that you already know how to put that much energy into a connection with someone. You have an abundance of energy, not only inside you, but also all around you. When you cut an aka connection, you can instantaneously bring all of that energy right back into the relationship. You can do it instantaneously, because it's all part of you. When

you disconnect with someone, you're allowing yourself to become pono, to forgive them, to have them forgive you, and to create a brand new connection, a bond that's even more special.

KEY POINTS ABOUT THE PROCESS

Ho'oponopono is something that needs to be practiced regularly. It amuses me when a student says, "OK, now I did it. Will I ever have to do it again?" That is like saying, "I had a salad tonight. Will I every have to eat healthy foods again?" Like a quick shower, ho'oponopono takes about 5 minutes and is probably something you want to do on a daily basis!

Be sure that the infinite source of love and healing continues to flow through you and to the person on the stage throughout the entire process. It's important that you experience the forgiveness both ways. You will know if the person doesn't respond with forgiveness; sometimes you'll hear it, you'll see it, or you'll just get a sense that there is resistance. If that happens, continue to flow the love, healing, energy from your heart to heal them. See that person as totally loved and totally healed up. Also, it is possible that the resistance signals that something needs to be said. Keep in mind that this is in your head, that you should be in charge of the answer, so say anything you need to. Allow full emotional disclosure to take place. Finally, there are occasions when students felt they needed to talk to the person they had brought on stage face-to-face. If that seems appropriate for you, please do arrange a direct conversation, always keeping yourself safe.

BECOMING PONO WITH OUR THREE SELVES

Remember that there is a connection between the conscious mind and the unconscious mind, and between the unconscious mind and the higher self. The question becomes, "What if I am not pono with my unconscious mind and higher self? Do I do ho'oponopono to become pono with these selves?" And the answer is, "No. It doesn't work that way."

First of all there is a natural disconnection of the selves at the end of one's life. But you would not want to disconnect while still alive. That would be like disconnecting from a part of your body. You just don't do that, not with parts of you as vital to living as the conscious mind, unconscious mind and higher self. But a student of mine tried it once. He did a ho'oponopono process with his unconscious mind. When he got to the step of cutting the aka connection with his unconscious, the blades wouldn't cut it. He emailed me, saying he was frustrated that he couldn't cut the connection. I emailed back telling him that he should feel lucky. The fact that the aka connection couldn't be cut meant that he was still alive!

I've never had someone tell me that they didn't feel pono with their higher conscious self. But I have had students tell me that they feel out of rapport or not pono with their unconscious self and therefore feel unable to connect with the higher self. This is precisely why we do the work we do: ho'oponopono to become pono with others, noa ("cleansing") of emotions that need to be released, noho ("drawing in") of the energy of the higher self.

This is the work that makes you pono with yourself. Your three selves are who you are, and there's no quick and easy way to just put one of your minds on the stage to become pono with it. When you don't feel pono with yourself, it's a signal that you need to do some of the other work (ho'oponopono, noa, or noho).

How do we know we're not pono with the unconscious mind if it's unconscious? You know you're not pono with the unconscious mind when the unconscious mind is not handling what it is supposed to do as you would like. For instance, health issues are a sign that you are not pono with your unconscious since it is the unconscious mind's job to take care of the physical body, to protect it and to keep it in good health. Milton Erickson, an M.D. who did hypnosis and hypnotherapy for years said, "Patients are patients because they are out of rapport with their unconscious mind." When someone experiences physiological disease or illness, there's a lack of rapport between conscious and unconscious. When you have a goal that you would like to achieve, but remain stuck or find yourself headed in the opposite direction from your goal, there's a lack of rapport with the unconscious mind.

There are a lot of different ways that it could show up. But it's not a question of being out of rapport or in rapport. Pono or rapport runs along a spectrum. So the question is, how much rapport do you have? Your unconscious mind is like a 5 to 7 year old child who loves you and wants to support you. The unihipili may have become confused because the connection with the conscious was not as strong as it should be. It's like the people in our lives. With some of them, we hardly have to say a word to be understood. With others, it's almost as if you are speaking different languages; no matter how often you say something, they don't get it!

If your unihipili (unconscious) is not getting it, it's the conscious mind that is responsible for cleaning up the communication and building rapport. When I first discussed these selves in Chapter Four, I mentioned that the conscious needs to learn to treat the unconscious as the higher self treats it, with loving respect. That's when you really become pono with yourself.

You may experience yourself as just a conscious mind and that you are only present consciously. But the unconscious mind and the higher self are always active, always doing their jobs as defined by their prime directives. When you experience pono and feel harmony with all three selves, the unconscious mind tends to the physical, allowing energy to flow and systems to work smoothly. When important information comes in, the unconscious mind retains it for you. The higher consciousness provides energy you need and wise guidance to assist the instinct and intuition offered by the unconscious mind. Allowed to work properly, these minds ensure not only physical health, but emotional well-being as well.

WHEN TO START HO'OPONOPONO?

My best suggestion is to take some time while the information is still fresh to do the process on your own. I know it works from my research, and I have experienced it working with thousands of people. (I have CDs available which guide you through the process with an individual and another which details a more global process to forgive and release all of the people with whom you are connected. Find them at www.Huna.com or email info@huna.com)

SUMMARY:

1. Ho'oponopono requires mutual forgiveness.

2. The Hawaiians believed that everything must be forgiven – no exceptions.

3. Done regularly, ho'oponopono can contribute greatly to your feeling pono with others and yourself.

CHAPTER TWELVE: EMOTIONAL HEALTH

When the missionaries arrived in the mid-nineteenth century, the Hawaiians they found on the islands had few if any psychological or physiological ailments. The Hawaiian culture at that time viewed mind and body as integrally related and had several approaches to health that were integrated into their lives and practiced by the Kahuna of healing. This system that was integrated in the treatment of dis-ease helped to promote the Hawaiian paradise.

THE BLACK BAG

Papa Bray taught a beautiful metaphor for one aspect of maintaining a healthy mind-body connection. When individuals had an experience but didn't have the tools to deal with it in the moment, or if they didn't know how or weren't ready to release the emotions connected with it, the unconscious, unihipili, took that experience and put it into a metaphorical black bag.

They then closed that black bag and stashed it somewhere in the body until the person was equipped or ready to release it.

Take for example the death of a loved one. Emotions that death evokes can be overwhelming to handle initially. Every culture has a different view on the appropriate amount of time for grieving and an appropriate form of expression. If you would not or could not release those emotions appropriately for any reason, unihipili stored them into a black bag until the time was right for you. The Hawaiians believed that at some point, either consciously or unconsciously, you would know that it was time to release the experience that had been stuffed into your black bag.

If the realization is conscious, the Huna system has a process for internal self therapy or higher self release. As they did in ancient days, you can visit a volcano and symbolically take all of your black bags out and throw them into the volcano to be destroyed, as Uncle George once described. This would be an example of an external release. The fire element is helpful with transformation and change, so visiting a site that is connected with that element is a form of release. Because "as above, so below" is so powerful, what happens or exists outside, happens and exists inside as well. The external expression (above) affects the internal (below). With guidance from your higher self and some focus, the negative emotion can be released and everything made pono within you again inside, no matter what you are dealing with.

Sometimes, however, your unconscious mind, unihipili, decides, "You're ready to let it go." The bag opens and all of the emotions and experiences are relived so they can dissipate. This can happen anytime. We've all experienced having a good day when out of nowhere and for no apparent reason, sadness bubbles up. Papa Bray said this is a signal from unihipili that "You're ready to let it go," so it is perfect to express the emotion. In ancient times, if Hawaiians felt sad, they would weep; if they felt anger bubble up, they would express it and allow it to dissipate. As they did so, they knew it was natural and expressed gratitude for the release. They had faith that unihipili knew when the time was right and trusted that they had the tools and techniques to handle it. They would release the black bag and move forward.

This points out a difference between Western society and the ancient system of Huna. In the West, when negative emotions surface out of nowhere, we panic. We don't see the upheaval as a positive signal from the unconscious that we are ready to resolve the issue, but rather a signal that something is wrong with us. We medicate, we deny, and we avoid. We push those feelings back down below the surface.

To the Huna way of thinking, this only confuses the unconscious mind. Unihipili is working hard to preserve the body, to release anything that could upset the mind-body balance. The unconscious mind knows that you need to remove the black bag of unreleased negative thoughts and feelings from your neurology before it makes you sick. It can't understand why you won't let that black bag go.

Your unconscious hears you saying, "I want to be happy." So your unconscious mind replies, "Then let go of your sadness." "No," you insist, "I don't want to be sad, I want to be happy." And your unconscious mind repeats, "Okay, then let go of your sadness." You are annoyed now. "There must be something wrong here. I don't want sadness, I want happiness!" Eventually the unconscious mind gives up: "Oy vey. Do what you want!"

In Huna, we purposely let go. If a black bag comes up, we are taught to thank our unconscious mind, and honor ourselves by trusting that we have what we need to move through it and let it go. Releasing the black bags is a form of higher self therapy. The higher self enters the body and the unconscious mind and pulls the black bags out. You don't have to know what's in your bags. It's not our conscious mind's job to remember all the times that you were angry or specifically what made you sad. All the conscious mind has to do is give the higher self permission.

The unconscious mind and the higher self only operate with permission from the conscious mind. A person's conscious mind can deny the existence of the unconscious mind. It can even deny the existence of the higher self. But when permission is granted, the unconscious mind organizes the memories, holds those black bags for you, and signals you when the time for release is right. When you consciously decide that you are ready to release what should be released, the conscious mind invites the higher self in with the help of the awaiku (good spirits). All the conscious mind has to do is relax and let it happen, and be willing to let go. The higher self takes care of the rest. The conscious mind's job is to simply allow the other minds or selves to do their jobs. (Initiation to working with awaiku with others is presented in Level 2 of Huna training. In Level 1, students are taught to do the process with themselves. Visit www.Huna.com or email info@huna.com for a CD recording to guide you through the Level 1 process.)

It is not human nature for us to hold on to things because the prime directive of the unconscious mind is to let experiences go. Growing up, you may have been taught that you can't let go of certain issues or emotions quickly. This is your opportunity to change that belief.

My mom described my grandfather as a very forgiving person who would let go of any negative emotion as soon as it happened. Have you ever known someone like that? Or known the opposite? The simple question is: Which one do you want to be? It is possible to let go of things easily. It takes an incredible amount of energy to hold onto feelings that are no longer useful for us. What else could you create in your life with the energy that is now dedicated to holding onto what you no longer need?

BLACK BAGS IN THE BODY

With modern technology, these black bags can now be measured. In the book Foundation Theory, Dr. Paul Goodwin explains how these black bags can be measured along neuro pathways. He describes how, by using electrical impulses along neural pathways, these repressed emotions show up as blockages along the pathways, and that you can see the change in communication within the nervous system. Many massage therapists run into these black bags as well. While massaging certain problem areas in a client's body, that client might re-experience a wave of old emotions and feel a physical as well as emotional release. The emotions within the black bag had formed a physical blockage or issue. Releasing that physical blockage can help release the emotional black bag as well.

Black bags tend to go where you direct them to go by your language. What do I mean by that? Someone who doesn't like their job and continually says "This job is a pain in the neck" might suffer from difficulty in the neck or head. Any time he or she has a negative experience at work, the unconscious mind puts the black bag exactly where instructed. Unihipili likes instructions. It's one of the prime directives. Therefore it's important to be aware of your language. If you habitually use phrases like, "I have a heavy heart because of that situation," enough black bags will accumulate in that area to create a profound physiological affect.

Comments that connect emotions with body symptoms are either giving the unconscious mind instructions, or they're expressing how someone experiences the black bags. Psychological studies have shown that certain emotions have more impact on the heart, for example. Many articles published in the Journal of the American Medical Association relate anger to heart-related issues. The entire focus of the discipline in psychology called PNI (psychoneuroimmunology) focuses on studying how specific stressors affect specific areas of the body. Dr. Deepak Chopra is one of the founders of PNI and is credited with early research in this area. This is key: If you never tell the black bags where to go, unihipili will spread them out evenly rather than letting them pile up in one area.

ARE NEGATIVE EMOTIONS BAD?

Another important question is whether negative emotions are bad. I don't believe they are. Negative emotions like anger, sadness, fear and guilt provide us with feedback about our surroundings and our experiences. If every time you walk into a certain location, you feel fear, that's a clue! Don't go there!

What Huna proposes is that holding on to the negative emotions past the point where they are ready for a natural release is unhealthy for the mind, body and spirit. That release is our focus when we do ho'oku'u or higher self therapy.

EMOTIONAL BODY/WATER ELEMENT

The water element is related to the emotional body. Water at a metaphysical level is magnetic. It draws in energy or repels energy, depending on what you hold in your emotional body. Your emotional body is related to your unconscious mind. Therefore, a person who has a lot of repressed anger activates the water element via emotions. The water in the emotional body magnetizes the anger energy and actually draws more anger to it. Haven't you known people who are always angry and seem to attract angry situations into their lives? If you push fear down into your emotional body, the water charges up with fear and pulls in truly frightening circumstances. It pulls danger to you like a magnet. Given this, what types of emotions do you want to store? The emotional body will take your lead and attract more of the same.

> We pile new energies and emotions on top of old ones, and wonder why new circumstances end up feeling much the same as in the past. The black bags turn into baggage!

If you want to fill your emotional body with love so that you attract love, you need to noa (cleanse) the negative emotions first. On the physical level, most of us are naturally motivated to do some form of cleansing before we bring in something new. We shower before we go on a date. We clean the house when guests are due. We wash our food before we eat it.

But in many cultures, we neglect to do this emotionally. We remarry while still carrying the pain and anger of past relationships. We start a new job still wounded by our failure in the last one. We view our children through the fears of our own childhoods. We pile new energies and emotions on top of old ones, and wonder why new circumstances end up feeling much the same as in the past. The black bags turn into baggage!

Huna teaches that it's just as important to noa (cleanse) on the emotional level and mental level as on the physical. If we noa first before we noho (bring down) a new energy, we're able to direct it. Noa allows us to cleanse so we are able to noho and move and direct energy from a place of aloha, from the heart.

BEGINNING CLEANSING

The ho'oku'u process is a guided process that has helped hundreds and thousands of people. Once I teach people, I always say they now know, and have a responsibility to practice it anytime something comes up. At level 2 of our Huna workshop, we initiate haumana (students) with awaiku (good spirits) to help them work with others. This book provides a way for you to begin to tap into this. If you are interested in studying level 2, please visit http://www.Huna.com for upcoming courses.

Papa Bray would say that the worst thing to do is hold onto the black bag because it would just build up. Like our volcano here in Hawai'i, if it is not continuously erupting (as it has been for about 20 years now) then there will be a problem, eventually an explosion. Constant release keeps the volcano from blowing its top.

Just like an active volcano, you can begin to practice what Papa taught my father, and what psychology calls emotional disclosure. It means to talk or write about it. Studies have shown clearly that by talking or writing about a negative situation, the negative affect and bad feelings are reduced. We tend to make issues worse in our minds. Have you ever held something in, gnawed on it until it felt worse? When you do finally blow and let it out, you often realize that it wasn't that big a deal.

Here is how to begin. Ask a loved one or friend if you can vent with him or her. Asking permission is preferable to just springing it on someone and possibly making them feel as if they had done something wrong. Ask them for a time where you can vent, let out what is bothering you, and let them know it is about you, and not them. Make sure you do this in a space that is appropriate.

I met a couple in Toronto in one of my workshops who were having marital problems and who had heard me teach this venting process. They told me they were considering a separation. When I asked where they were venting — they said in bed! I explained that spaces in our homes and in our lives are made for certain types of energy. The bed is not usually the place to vent. I asked them to suggest a better place, and they decided to try the living room. By changing where they practiced venting for just a week, they found that love and intimacy came back into their relationship. This happened because energetically we want to release our negativity. We simply need to find the right space and time to do it.

Negativity and Doubt

Our black bags contain not only negative emotions but also the self-imposed limitations of negativity and doubt that come from the mental plane. The mental body listens to your conscious limiting beliefs about who you are and what you can do. So, if you don't think you can be happy, the mental body ensures that you are correct.

Doubts are limiting decisions and/or limiting beliefs about yourself and your abilities. Self-doubt manifests in words like "I can't," "I'm not good enough," "I'm not smart enough," or "I am not spiritual enough." Limiting decisions usually live in the mental body. They have less emotional quality though they may be strongly held. As you light up these doubts in your neurology, the black bags will feel a little bit different. The flavor is more mental than emotional, though some limiting decisions and beliefs have an emotional aspect as well.

Why "Black" Bag?

Papa Bray said that the color black was used because in life we progress down a path. Whether that path is an aim in life to be healthy or more spiritual, or if the path is a specific goal of creating an amazing relationship or reaching a specific weight, the path to get from the idea of what we desire to the desired goal itself is the path we travel.

When we literally walk down a path, we need one very important thing. When I ask students in my workshops what that very important thing might be, they respond with things like "resources" or "friends." But it's even simpler than that: You need light! When you walk down a path, you need to have enough light to see where to place your next step. The color black was used for our black bags because black or darkness is the absence of the light.

When you have negative emotions or limiting decisions stored up in black bags and you attempt to go down a path, the darkness of the bags prevents you from seeing where you need to go or what you need to do. They cloud our judgment and sometimes make us take a misstep. For example, my fear prevented me from starting a weight reduction program for many years. Every time I thought of doing it, I couldn't even see how to start. Many of us feel like we are stumbling around "in the dark" at some point or other. This is the effect of maintaining those black bags beyond their usefulness. It is the release of these negative emotions that allows the light to shine and illuminate our path.

BEGIN YOUR RELEASE PROCESS!

The best advice I can give you is to schedule the time to release now. Call your friend, talk to your partner, ask him or her if you could make a time and space to just let some things out. As an energy exchange, you could give them some time and space to do the same. Schedule it now, while you are thinking about it, because you will be more likely to do it if it is on your calendar.

SUMMARY:

1. In many ways, letting go of negativity is even more important to emotional well-being than embracing the positive.

2. Hanging on to black bags beyond their usefulness can create not only emotional problems but physical problems as well.

3. Our unconscious will signal when it is time to release a black bag. All we need to do is go with the flow.

CHAPTER THIRTEEN: SPIRITUALITY & MATERIAL LIFE

Unlike some other paths, Huna teaches that it is okay to be successful and spiritual at the same time. Poverty or the lack of success has nothing to do with spirituality. You don't need to give up everything in your life or all of worldly possessions to prove your spirituality. Some of my greatest teachers have been some of the most successful people I've ever met. But success doesn't necessarily mean that you have the most money in the bank. Success means that you are surrounded by wealth and abundance, and you get to define what wealth and abundance are.

In my mind, any training in esoteric studies should enhance our positive character traits and above all, it should bring balance and peace of mind. If it doesn't, there's something wrong. What could possibly be the purpose of experiencing the heavens opening up to us and yet lose our reason, livelihood, and friends? To put it clearly, training in Huna should not cause

someone to lose his job, relationships, and all that is dear to him. Remember that you have four bodies: physical, emotional, intellectual, and spiritual. Training should take into account all four of these and bring them into balance to produce stability and harmony in life.

Dion Fortune was an esoteric writer from the 20th century. She said that "the descent into matter had to be complete before the ascent to spirit could begin." This means that you need to learn how to accept and be in charge of the physical. Before the ascent to spirit can begin, the descent into matter has to be complete. So it is not only possible, but it is necessary to be both successful on the physical plane (according to your definition of success) and spiritual.

Some teachers teach that the physical is evil, dirty or nasty. But the physical is our foundation and our stability. Huna teaches that everything physical flows from the spiritual. Therefore, it can't be evil, dirty, or nasty based on its source. I believe that we have been out of balance for sometime now with our physical surroundings, our planet, and our physical bodies. Many people in America are overweight, and our planet could be in much better shape. The attitude that the physical is evil, dirty and nasty may have even contributed to this. John Ka'imikaua explained that Hawaiian's believed the aina (the land) was perfect and that a harmony should be created between you and your environment.

Hula Dancers

According to Etua, in hula every time you learn a new movement, you're given a new pohaku (stone). To become a hula dancer, you take each pohaku and you build a foundation. Someday when you have enough of those stones and have learned enough movements and their nuances, you will have a solid foundation to dance upon. So it is with building a foundation in the physical plane. When you flow energy, you're either directing it toward the creation of the things that you need on the physical realm, or you're directing it toward moving from the physical realm to the spiritual. But before you begin to move to spirit, you need that physical foundation.

When I was a child spending time with the yogi Baba Muktananda, the Indian swami who brought siddha yoga to the West, he told the story of how he woke up one day and realized, "My dharma (purpose or life path) is to go teach this siddha yoga in the Western speaking world." In order to do that, he needed to create wealth. He had to manifest the resources to do what he was being led to do. He created a foundation and soon had millions of dollars in it. He had no attachment to the money yet it allowed him to travel wherever he needed to go and do the work he was called to do.

Baba was approached once by a student who said, "I haven't learned how to create enough resources for my family. What's the problem?" Baba replied, "You don't have enough shakti (energy)." The man hadn't learned how to channel enough energy yet and that was reflected in his lack of physical resources.

THE FOUR BODIES

In addition to coming to peace with money, you also need to be okay with your physical body. You have to become pono with the fact that you have one. I've met people whose desire to be spiritual is so strong that they say, "I want to disconnect from my physical." We were given a physical body for a reason and since you have one, the real question is what are you doing with it?

Huna makes a distinction between the four bodies but it does not see them as separate. In other words, all four bodies are you and all bodies are to be honored and evolved. So to deny your emotional body and seek to have no emotions in the quest of spirituality makes no more sense to Huna practitioners than denying your mental body and going insane! Instead, the spiritual path of Huna involves mastering all four bodies and all three selves. As Dion Fortune said, "Unless the study of esoteric science yields fruits of practical application, it is unworthy of the pursuit of any serious minded person, and unless these fruits be the fruits of the spirit, it is unworthy of the study of any spiritually minded person." In other words, the spiritual plane and the physical plane are interwoven. To try to exist exclusively on one plane and deny the other does not serve you.

FOCUS

However, you need to figure out where you are on your path and what needs work. Do you need to focus on aligning your emotional body? Improve your understanding and relationship with the unconscious? Do you need to build your foundation of material resources? In which direction are you focusing right now? Become pono with that. And make sure that the spiritual, mental, emotional and physical bodies are

in alignment with the path you are on, the path that is right for you.

In life, without focus, you wander aimlessly and get whatever it is that you get. When you have a focus, when you have a direction, then you are moving toward something and you know whether or not you are on track. In every area of your life, with everything that you do, it is so important to ask yourself, "Why am I here? What do I want to achieve?" I often attend trainings or read to expand my knowledge. When I do, I ask the same questions: "Why am I here or reading this? What do I want to achieve?" It really enhances my absorption and understanding of whatever teaching is before me.

Huna teaches that the universe has infinite knowledge. Therefore you can never hope to learn everything, and that's a good thing. So understanding the infinite knowledge of the universe is an aim, never an end. To me, the study of Huna is an aim, spirituality is an aim. In contrast, in career or physical development, you might have end goals.

Relationship is also an aim. You might begin with an initial end goal of getting into a relationship. But once you are in one, you have to switch your thinking because relationship is a constant journey that requires a direction (i.e. an aim).

My aim is to learn how to play god in my own universe, to learn how to tap into my own higher conscious mind. I know that areas in my life need improvement. In many ways, I see my life as perfect. But perfection seeks to outdo itself. Did you ever notice that? Have you have ever had a goal, a desire or level of achievement that makes you say, "If I just get this particular thing or get to that particular level, my life will be perfect." What happens as soon as you get there? You set a new goal and you take it to the next level. When all four bodies and three minds are in alignment, these physical, emotional, or mental goals move us along the path in the direction of our aim toward higher conscious mind.

> # When you are following your heart and doing what you love to do it's not called work, it feels like it is a part of your life.

MASTERY VERSUS SPIRITUALITY

There are two different types of magic. There's magic with a C, which refers to the guy who creates illusions with smoke and mirrors and does card tricks. Then there's magic with a K, which is Western hermetic magik. Magik is most often associated with the "lesson of mastery." Much of the focus of magik is taking the same principles I've outlined in this book and applying them to creating things on the physical level. The lesson of mastery means learning how to become in charge of your projections.

There is a trickle down effect as we have talked about previously. In life, we get a spark or some energy to do something. It is like an "a-ha" where

we feel as if we just woke up to something. That moves the mana into the mental body. There we begin to think about it and what we want to do. At some point, we become motivated by these thoughts, and that is the mana in the emotional body. This energy builds up until we finally do something! Each step is taking the energy from the spiritual and bringing it down into the physical. This is magik or what Papa Bray referred to as the lesson of mastery. That is, mastering, or moving the energy down into the physical to learn how to create your foundation.

In one, or even more than one, area of your life, you may need to do this. I had to with my health. I had an idea of what I wanted, however, I had not brought it down into the physical. I had not manifested or mastered my own health. Some need to do this in career; they may have been unable to generate the income needed to do things that are empowering or even relaxing. Others may need to focus on relationships.

Whatever it is, the lesson of mastery is about creating a foundation in each area so you are able to rise up to spirit once again (which Papa Bray called the "lesson of life").

CONSCIOUSNESS TO THE PHYSICAL

Many of us do the teaching we do because we know we can affect the overall consciousness of people, which in turn will change the overall consciousness of society, which in turn will continue to empower the planet.

Others of us feel called to go directly to troubled areas of the planet and do counseling or physical work to make a contribution. Both are good and both are effective. The important point is to determine what it is you are to do, and simultaneously let go of what you think others should do. See the planet as perfect and then decide what it is you need to do. And if you have any desire to do something, you have to do it. When you are following your heart and doing what you love to do it's not called work, it feels like it is a part of your life.

SUMMARY:

1. Spiritual development is not separate from, but includes the physical, material world.

2. Our job is to bring all four bodies and all three minds into balance.

3. All paths are valid and following your true calling is your unique contribution to the planet.

Epilogue

A ʻOHE PAU KO IKE I KOU HALAU

I meet lots of people around the world who have experienced various spiritual and scientific truths. Sometimes they say, "I heard you study Huna but you should study what I'm learning because it's better."

One of my kumu ("teachers") Uncle George Naʻope had a phrase above his Hula school that I saw when I went to live with him for a summer in '93: A ohe pau ko ike i kou halau. The rough English translation is, "Think not that all wisdom is in your school." It was a reminder that there are other ways of thinking, there are other ways of doing things, there are other paths to the light. Huna is just one way. Uncle explained that this phrase creates a level of mutual respect allowing you to realize that you're just sharing ideas and concepts.

In this book, I'm sharing the information. But I often participate as a student to other teachers. And I put aside my thinking because I know that what they share will enhance my own path, my own approach to the light. I have a great deal of respect for other approaches, other traditions, and other teachings. I'm simply sharing one path, one concept that can resonate with individuals regardless of their current beliefs.

After my father published the book Timeline Therapy and the Basis of Personality,[1] a student in an ashram in India wrote to him saying, "This timeline that you've talked about here, the timeline – we believe you have found the resting place that resides in every individual that stores the akashic records. And I think that you have tapped into one of very few techniques that release negative emotions (like higher self therapy does) that allows you to then release karma that might take a few lifetimes to do." Even in an ancient system in a far away ashram, sincere students were able to glean benefit from a different teaching.

James, T., & Woodsmall, W. (1988). Time Line Therapy and the Basis of Personality. Capitola, CA: Meta Publications.

119

Personally, I realized that eventually you have to pick a path. You have to make the commitment. When I finally found my path in Huna, I stayed on that path. Sometimes we spend too much time thinking the grass is greener over there, or that another philosophy or religion will solve our problems. Instead, if you can find new information and incorporate it into your chosen path, your travel will become easier. You don't have to jump the track and follow a new path. Comparing paths is unproductive.

When I finally found my path in Huna, I stayed on that path.

You can be good at a lot of things, or you can master one. When Etua was first dancing hula, he learned how to dance many forms of Polynesian dance. Etua had a gift and was able to see someone do one quick move then learn it instantly. He performed in Las Vegas, Reno, and traveled around the world. One day, a master came up to him and said, "You have an opportunity. You're going to do one of two things in your lifetime. You're going to be really good at a lot of things, or you'll be a master at one thing."

IT'S A PROCESS

The spirit of any esoteric training does not lie solely in the information being shared, but in the influences that come from the teacher which, over time, tune the student to higher and higher levels of vibration. An esoteric teaching is different from other studies. Its intent is to communicate wisdom, but its real power lies in contacts with the unseen and inner worlds. Without these contacts, students can't put the intellectual theory into practice. All of the different schools of the original teachings generally share the same principles but they differ very much in how they gather their power and in their ability to apply and share that power.

There are very few things that still make me sad, with the exception of profound loss, of course. But one thing that saddens me is when a student begins to study Huna then experiences a negative emotion and concludes, "Oh, that Huna stuff didn't work because I'm still having negative emotion." That student missed the point.

Huna doesn't make your life perfect, only you can make your life perfect. Huna is a tool and a technique for empowerment. Like any tool, if you take this information and put it on shelf, it'll just sit there. Huna is more than the words contained in this book. If you work with its concepts and practices on a regular basis, one day you'll experience a negative emotion and instantly recognize, "I have the tools and techniques to deal with this."

I've been doing this work since I was five years old. Is my life perfect? Well, I think it is, but not because it is without issues, problems to solve or emotions to release. It's perfect because I have incorporated Huna into my daily life, my way of being. Huna allows me to feel pono more often than not, but it still requires that I pay attention and work with the practices.

That's ahonui, patient perseverance. Pick a path and delve into it. Sometimes we just skim the pond, thinking that the next pond will be better. Whatever pond you choose, it will be much more rewarding to go deeply into that pond. I promise.

GLOSSARY

The language of Hawai'i expresses the concepts and basic principles of Huna with subtleties that are difficult to translate into English. To understand the deeper meanings of Hawaiian words, it's a common practice to divide them into their components in various ways. Please also note, that within a translation dictionary, there are multiple meanings to Hawaiian words. The explanations below are based on teachings from Uncle George, Papa Bray, as well as the spiritual meanings of the words.

Ahi: the fire element; includes light, heat, red, sun

Ahonui: patient perseverance

Aina: land or environment

Aka: connection; literally "sticky stuff"; the etheric substance that is a conduit for mana or energy

Akua: a god or the essential energy of something

Aloha: from the heart; a state of mind and being

A = Ao: light, to move toward enlightenment

L = Lokahi: oneness, unity

O = 'Oia'i'o: truth, to be truthful

H = Ha'a ha'a : humility; to be humble

A = Aloha: absolute, true love

Aumakua: higher conscious mind

Awaiku: good spirits

Ha: breath that comes from inside you

Ha'a ha'a: humility; to be humble

Hala: to miss the right path; to err by omission

Haumana: students

Hawai'i: the supreme life force that rides on the breath

Hawaiiana: the Hawaiian culture, or spirituality

Hewa: going overboard, to err by excess

Honua: the earth element; literally earth

Ho'omana: one of the original names for Huna; empowerment or to empower

Ho'o: to make

Ho'oponopono: to make pono; the Hawaiian forgiveness process

Huna: esoteric knowledge which is hidden from view or concealed; wisdom which is "protected like a treasure."

I: supreme

Imu: oven, a cauldron; the "oven" of the body below the belly button; solar plexus

Ino: To do intentional harm with hate or ill intent

Kahuna: a master or expert in a particular knowledge, comparable to a very learned PhD

Kahuna ho'omana: Kahuna of healing

Kane: creator of the universe, masculine aspect, outer expression of higher self

Kapu: ancient religious system of taboos

Keawe: One source; God

Kilokilo: branch of Huna that focuses on divination

Ku: God of war, outer expression of subconscious mind

Kumu: teacher

Kumulipo: ancient manuscript or teaching of creation

La'au Kahea: branch of healing that focuses on psychological healing and an ability to call the energies / elements

La'au Lapa'au: Kahuna specializing in medicine

Lalo: below; physical plane

Lele: wind

Lokahi: oneness, unity

Luna: above; spiritual plane

Makani: air element; external breeze or wind

Malama: to cherish

Mana: basic life-force; energy; ki, chi, shakti

Manamana: conscious energy related to the conscious mind or focus

Mana loa: 3rd or highest level of vibration or energy, sacred or spiritual energy of the higher self

Mana'o: personal reality or perspective

Mea aloha: beloved

Na'auao: mystical initiators of Huna

Noa: to cleanse

Noho: to draw in (down) or bring in

'Oia'i'o: truth, to be truthful; genuine, authentic.

Oli: to chant

Po: deep nothingness

Pohaku: a stone; part of a foundation

Pono: a state of being in alignment with higher consciousness; the sense of being right with yourself and the world

Pule: prayer; calling on the energies or gods for cooperation based on the connectedness of everything

Uhane: conscious mind

Uli: feminine aspect necessary for creation

Unihipili: unconscious mind

Wahine: female

Wai: water element, mana, life force

ABOUT THE AUTHOR

Matthew B. James, Ph.D., international trainer, lecturer, and educator, embodies the principles he teaches. While devoting himself to his integrity, Dr. James has built an international firm dedicated to personal transformation and heads a university which provides in-depth education in consciousness studies. Throughout his work, Dr. James weaves effective modern technologies with timeless ancient wisdom.

Dr. James has been immersed in spiritual studies and the science of human potential since the age of five. He began his training in childhood, learning meditation and siddha yoga directly from such teachers as Baba Muktananda, as well as studying Huna, the primordial science of consciousness of Hawaii, from Uncle George Na'ope. In the 80's, Dr. James studied directly with several well-known teachers in the human potential movement, including Tony Robbins and Richard Bandler. In the last fifteen years, Dr. James has become the Trainer of Trainers himself. Chris Howard and many other prominent trainers have spent time studying with his organization, learning both the modern techniques for personal transformation and the ancient practices of Huna.

Dr. James is President of The Empowerment Partnership, a firm that delivers transformational seminars and intensive trainings throughout the US, Canada, Asia, and Europe.

Most importantly, Dr. James has the honor and responsibility of carrying on the lineage of Kuauhaoali'i Huna. He has been a student of Huna, the ancient science of consciousness and energy healing of Hawaii, since the early 80's. The lineage Dr James continues includes the Bray family and the spiritual teachings Uncle George Na'ope (named by the State of Hawaii as a Golden Living Treasure). Dr. James is committed to teaching the Huna tradition, fully and undiluted, to as many students as are called to it.

Dr. James' degrees include a Master's in Organizational Management, a Doctorate in Clinical Hypnotherapy, and a Ph.D. in Health Psychology.

 www.huna.com

CPSIA information can be obtained
at www.ICGtesting.com
Printed in the USA
BVOW02s1132071216

470050BV00003B/20/P